"INDIAN GAME,"

(FROM QUAIL TIGER)

"INDIAN GAME,"

(FROM QUAIL TIGER)

WILLIAM RICE

GYAN

Published by

GYAN

Gyan Publishing House
5, Ansari Road
Daryaganj, New Delhi-110002
Phone: 011-47034999, 9811692060
E-mail: books@gyanbooks.com

Distribution Network
gyanbooks.com
India, USA, Canada, UK, Australia

ISBN: 978-93-6433-249-1 (PB)
First Published, 1884

2nd Impression 2024

Printed at: Gyan Press, Delhi.

"INDIAN GAME," (FROM QUAIL TIGER)
Author: WILLIAM RICE

Maj. Gen. W. Rice, Delt. Shaw & Sons, Lith.

"GAVÆUS GAURUS"_ INDIAN WILD BULL OR BISON ("KHULGA").

"INDIAN GAME,"

(FROM QUAIL TO TIGER.)

BY WILLIAM RICE,

Major-General, Retired List, Indian Army.

"'Unting is all that's worth living for. All time is lost wot is not spent in 'unting."
—JOHN JORROCKS, Esq. (some time Master of the "Handley Cross" Fox Hounds.)

LONDON:
PUBLISHED BY W. H. ALLEN & CO., WATERLOO PLACE, PALL MALL, W.

1884.

PREFACE

HAVING written a book called "Tiger Shooting in India," published in 1857, which at the time was not unfavourably received, the Author has now added, in the following pages, full descriptions of very many other kinds of game, both great and small, so that the whole may form a sort of "Guide for Beginners," or "griffin's" *vade mecum* in the noble art of "Shikar," as well as affording to those at home (who may care for the subject) some idea of the sport obtainable in India. These experiences do not extend beyond the Bombay Presidency; but that, being nearest to England, will probably form the first "happy hunting ground" of most new arrivals, or sportsmen strange to the country. Thinking that possibly such a work may soon be in demand (regard being had to the increasing scarcity of game at home), a beginning shall at once be made, without further apology to the reader of these random notes.

First shall be noticed the amusement afforded by the shot or "scatter gun" of our American friends, ere we proceed to the glorious performances of India's own weapon—the rifle, so that the novice will be led by degrees up to Tiger Shooting, which subject will be described towards the end of these pages, and some few scenes mentioned in the Book of 1857 will be re-produced therein as cautions to beginners.

W. R.

April, 1884.

CHAPTER I.

SMALL GAME SHOOTING.

Beating across Country for Small Game—Quail Shooting—Partridges of divers sorts—Sand Grouse—Florikin Shooting—Houbara—Bustard Hares—White Foxes.

(*Plate I. shows a party of four guns, but of course any number can join, engaged in beating across country towards some village, where their small tents have been previously sent on.*)

This sport is usually commenced in the early morning, for then the game is easier to start than during the noontide heat, besides being the most pleasant time of the day; moreover the ground has not been disturbed by scattered herds of grazing cattle or peasants going to or at their work.

Still in the cold season a start can be made later on in the morning if preferred.

As many men or beaters having been collected as are required, six or eight often being allowed between each gun, especially at starting, for some will very soon be required to fall behind, to either carry the game or assist in looking for wounded or lost birds, a line is formed, and the whole party set off, each beater being armed with a long stick of bamboo to beat every bush in passing. All endeavour to keep in as straight a line as possible, and at equal distances of about three or four paces apart, moving slowly forward.

The shooters regulate the pace, which depends chiefly on the amount of game flushed, and the nature of the ground and they also see that the beaters keep their proper places, not lagging behind and so letting the game escape past them, or pushing on dangerously in front of the guns.

Over tolerably open rocky ground the men merely tap a stone now and then in passing, or by gently calling out or grunting merely at intervals, while slowly strolling along, start whatever game there may be found, their presence alone then being sufficient to scare it; too much noise is sometimes a mistake, as being likely to put up objects out of gunshot. Only hares are here generally to be met with, but among low bushes a closer formation is required, so as not to pass over any lurking game.

In grain fields, especially where quail are at all plentiful, very careful, steady, slow beating is needed.

The men either join hands or hold on to a stick apiece, so as not to unnecessarily damage the crops; mere walking so, without trampling through fields, does not hurt the low corn or barley in a more or less unripe state, so is seldom objected to by the cultivators.

The sport now is truly delightful, an almost incessant firing is kept up as the quail are roused a few paces only in front of each gun, for the birds will lie close enough in these grain fields, no such good cover or shelter being perhaps forthcoming for them in the surrounding country.

The beaters mark well where each bird shot has dropped, and on passing, pick it up, very rarely indeed failing to so retrieve a fallen bird, no matter how dense the grain or cover may be, for all well-trained beaters, from constant practice, are most expert at this difficult business.

It would never do for any one to run forward to recover the game at the moment of its being shot, for by so doing, most likely, half a dozen other birds would be flushed and lost, for who can fire with any one in front of the gun?

Sometimes a few minutes may be lost in seeking wounded

birds, but the line can well afford to wait a little for breathing time, or to refill the bags emptied of cartridges, arrange any change required in the direction of the beat, or for a quiet sip at the water bottle, cold tea, or its substitute!

Of course some birds are lost now and then, runners, or slightly hit ones.

On finding and picking up the shot quail or partridges the men keep them for the time in their waistcloths, folded into a bag shape in front, for the purpose—such small birds to be afterwards collected and strung upon the shooting sticks.

Hares, florikin, peachicks, &c., would be at once passed along to be carried on bamboos by other men following in rear of the line of beaters.

Overhead hawks of different sorts may be often seen keeping up with the guns, and occasionally pouncing down on any wounded bird, and making off with the same before it has fallen to the ground even.

Spare men, ponies, or a camel carry the game hastily slung on sticks, fitted up with leather or string loops for the purpose.

Game must not be heaped up together in a bag, for it would soon become tainted if not freely exposed to the wind and air. To describe the usual contents of the "bag" it will be necessary to enumerate nearly every sort of small game procurable, such as partridges, both "grey" and "painted," "grey" and "rain" quail, "sand grouse," two sorts, "florikin," "koolung" (commonly called "cullum"), peacocks, &c., &c., according to localities, and the hares aforesaid. The scientific and local native name of each animal and bird mentioned in these pages will be found in the Appendix, according to the works of the celebrated naturalist, Dr. Jerdon, entitled the "Mammals and Game Birds of India."

With regard to the grey quail a good morning's work would easily give thirty brace or more to each gun, but these birds being migratory, the sport of course depends very much on the season.

In some years they actually swarm, but at other times may prove comparatively scarce, so this sort of shooting is in fact merely a question of cartridges holding out long enough to make a "big bag." Full charges of powder are not required; rising as they mostly do, so very close to the gun, the birds are dropped with a pretty rebounding bump on the ground at about thirty yards distance, a $\frac{3}{4}$ oz. charge of "No. 8 or 9" shot being sufficient. Quail fly very swiftly indeed, with a delightful whirring noise and an awkward twisting or zigzag flight after getting away well on the wing; this sudden jerk or twist in their course to one side or the other, will cause even a good shot to occasionally fire into space, unintentionally enough, but it is the bird's only chance, for otherwise they fly exactly like miniature partridges, seldom, if ever, "towering" or rising above a yard or so from the ground, and going off straight. They are about one-third the size of the English partridge, and almost as good eating. The hen bird of the grey quail is decidedly the largest, and has not the dark brown bands or collar on the throat, which at once distinguishes the cock bird.

I have since shot a few brace of these grey quail in England, and was delighted at being able to compare and identify them with my dear old acquaintances of India.

When it is remembered that quail shooting can be carried on every day for at least three months of the cold weather, or best time of the year in India, from about 15th December to 15th March, some idea may be formed of this most enjoyable small game sport.

Quail can be shot to a dog, for I have often had very good sport alone with a steady spaniel, always setting out at dawn, for the quail will not rise after 8 o'clock a.m., or when the sun begins to get at all hot; besides there is then no scent, and the dog gets done up from the heat and cannot work.

The borders of large lakes or dried up "tanks," as pretty large ponds are called in India, where there is plenty of rough tangled undergrowth of weeds, reeds, high grass, dried rushes, &c., afford good cover for quail. One dog at a time is enough, for the "rises" are fast enough, and more dogs working together would distract the attention.

I have seen the quail put up so fast by one of my dogs that he disdained to bring to hand or retrieve less than two, three, or even four quail he had pouched, at each journey. These valuable pets are, however, so sure to come to grief from endless enemies (sun, snakes, alligators, &c.), that it is painful to even suggest their being used for this sport.

The little "rain quail" shooting which begins shortly after the monsoon has set in, and when the parched earth is again beautifully green with springing grass, and fields of newly sprouting grain, is a milder description of sport, and often merely an excuse for taking out a gun after it has been from necessity long lying idle during the first severe burst of the rainy season.

They are smaller birds than the grey quail, the cocks being prettily marked, with black breasts and small spots. Their incessant cry, at short intervals, of "wheet," "wheet," in the green corn fields tempts one, after an in-door life, to look them up, as much for exercise as amusement; when flushed, they fly straight and low, seldom over four feet high, and soon drop, after going about a hundred yards. Rushy grass-grown patches among open thorn bushes are their likeliest haunts or cover. They are never so numerous as the grey quail; so a dozen or twenty brace would be a fair bag for one gun. They are very fair eating. Here again small charges of shot and powder will be sufficient. Later on in the season these birds get mixed up with the swarms of grey quail, but they can be distinguished by their wing feathers, which are plain brown, while the grey quail has its "primaries," or large end feathers, at tip of its wings, marked with dark bars.

The very small "button quail" is somewhat scarce, and certainly not worth shooting. It is very difficult to flush in the first instance, and decidedly objects to rise or be put up again a second time. The equally small "jungle bush quail" is also worthless for shooting. They are very common and well known, for a family party of about a dozen have the habit of hiding very close in some thick bush or patch of grass, and, on being approached, of suddenly whirring off in all directions, with as startling an effect, to a novice, as old Mr. Brigg's cock pheasant or blazing firework!

During the beat or drive, the "francolin," or "painted partridge," will be often put up singly, generally to be followed by its mate, rising just in time for the second barrel. They are handsome birds, and, where at all plentiful, afford very pretty shooting, rising something like a "rocketer pheasant," and then going off straight. They are found chiefly in green corn fields, especially if any irrigation or flooding of the wheat fields is going on. Sugar cane patches are also a favourite spot, and should be well worked through, for often three or four brace may be picked up out of a very small piece of green cane. Large patches of high grass on the banks of nullahs or ravines and small rivers are very likely places to hold these birds. They are not very strong on the wing, and are easily shot, seldom giving any trouble to retrieve. They are not particularly good eating, being almost tasteless, but add greatly to the appearance of the "bag." Their call heard in the early morning is most peculiar,—a harsh, grating noise, not to be mistaken when once heard. The bird perches on some high stone or mound, and continues calling, generally before rain is likely to fall, and again towards sunset, other cock birds in the neighbourhood answering each other at intervals on all sides.

The "grey partridge," everywhere very common in India is not thought much of. It will be often started from thick bushes and hedges round the fields near villages ; it lies close but flies uncommonly strong, and requires to be well hit to be brought down, and will then generally run a long way, giving endless trouble to find. About five or six only are found in company, but not rising together as an English covey does, though the birds are very like the English ones to look at. It has a very shrill call, like the word "tea-kettle," "tea-kettle," "tea-kettle," uttered in breathless haste, and very loud. It makes a tremendous whirr on rising, but does not go far, and when scattered, after being disturbed or shot at, begins calling almost directly afterwards, to collect its dispersed companions.

No one thinks of eating these birds, for they are extremely tough and tasteless, but one's servants or the beaters are glad to take them, so they are not wasted when shot. The natives catch numbers of them in nets, and keep them in small cages as pets, like tame parrots.

The now rather scarce "black partridge" is a different bird altogether, and will be only found in Scinde, or, perhaps Cutch (of course, speaking with reference to the Bombay Presidency alone), but I have seen them on the river "Lonee," far north of Camp Deesa, while lion hunting. It is a very large handsome bird, with beautiful black plumage, much spotted with white on the breast. On rising it "towers" for a few yards, like a pheasant, and goes off straight afterwards, giving an easy shot, nor is it hard to kill. They are mostly found in patches of high grass near water, in sugar canes, and in the beds of rivers where there is thick cover, rising singly out of the low "jow," as the cypress or tamarisk jungle is called, also where there is plenty of high green cultivation. They are tender but not very good when cooked.

While thus beating across country, on open, sandy, stony parts, "sand grouse" will be constantly met with. There are three sorts: one very large, but rare, and two others with pin tails. The largest sort are chiefly to be found in Scinde. Of the others, one called the "pallas," has feathers quite over the toes, like a "ptarmigan," and the other, a very common sort, with a great deal of black plumage about the stomach. These birds are also called "rock pigeons," or "rock partridges," sometimes by mistake, and on sandy plains are very numerous. They squat or lie very close, and might be easily mistaken for stones until put up, when they require to be hit hard to bring down, being very strong on the wing. They are worth shooting, being good to eat, but tough, and require to be skinned before cooking.

By waiting over or near any water where these birds come down to drink, any number may be shot, for relays are constantly arriving in spite of the noise of the gun. Their call as they fly high overhead in scattered flocks, gives warning to the gunner to look out, who must shoot well in front, for their flight is swifter than it appears. These birds are supposed to be the quail that fed the Israelites in the desert.

According to locality, "peacocks" will be often met with. In some places they are very numerous and tame, living close to villages, and swarming round corn yards and stacks of grain. In many parts of India there is a strong religious prejudice against their being killed, and certainly there is no sport in shooting such a large, tough, tame bird, but occasionally they are to be met with far away from any villages, when a few "peachicks," about half-grown only, can be bagged at discretion, for they are tender and well worth cooking. "Guzerat Turkeys" is the nick-name they then pass under. A near shot should be selected, for they carry off a large charge, and will run any distance, after coming down with a bump enough to smash any other bird.

The "florikin" is decidedly the best bird worth firing at that will be met with during the morning's beat. They arrive soon after the "rains" commence in June, and remain through the cold season, being found in rushy swampy places and in high grass, scattered mostly over wide open plains, at intervals of a few hundred yards apart when at all numerous, but, like the grey quail, they are subject to good and bad seasons, being sometimes quite scarce. The cock bird is very handsome, standing about twenty inches high, with neck and under part of the body black, while the back is beautifully mottled, like the bustard. There are six curious, thin, upright turned feathers, with small tufts at the end, growing from the back of the bird's head, and curling upwards, most peculiar, and somewhat resembling the crest of a peacock, on which account the florikin is in some parts called the "kur-mor," or "grass peacock." The hen bird is the larger of the two, and of a very game-looking light brown colour, prettily marked with darker brown bars, and spots on the head, back, wings and tail, but has no crest feathers as in the cock bird.

As the line of beaters advances, an occasional florikin rises very gracefully, towering about twenty yards high before soaring off, but with no whirr or swiftness, so they are very easy birds to shoot, having a sort of owl-like flight, and are not strong on the wing, for a slight hit brings them down. They may be often killed at extraordinary distances by firing well ahead, as they are to be sometimes seen flying high, and coming down the wind at a great pace.

Nobody ever loses a chance of firing at florikin, for they are considered the best bird for the table of all India, being decidedly as game in taste as they are in look. On their first arrival they are much sought after, gunners working for them all day, in spite of the continued showers at that time of year.

The cock bird has a most peculiar habit of jumping up high in the air, quite straight, for seven or eight yards, at intervals, generally three or four times in rapid succession. This is done to attract the attention of the hen birds constantly passing overhead, for these latter seem to be of a wandering, roving nature, sailing down with the wind with great swiftness, at about sixty yards high, in search of food or nesting places. This conduct also helps to attract the sportsman's attention, for by marking well the exact spot in the high green grass where the cock bird was last seen jumping, and by hastening to the place, it may be often flushed and bagged; but sometimes on reaching the very spot, alone and silently as possible, the bird is nowhere to be found. You must now keep quite still, with a bright look-out all round while waiting, when presently its little black head will be seen peering round above the high grass for about a second or so only, and generally just beyond gun range, when it instantly disappears. Now stoop down as low as possible and run in to where the bird's head was last viewed, then suddenly stopping short and standing up, look well all round, with the gun at the "ready," when the florikin is almost certain to rise from some most unexpected quarter, yet within shot, for it has been making off at its best pace, through the thick wet grass, which it threads with marvellous celerity, but being invisible, it is impossible to guess in which direction the game will takewing on fancying itself safe out of gun-shot. This little dodge has helped me to many a bird that otherwise would have been no more seen, for they are cunning enough to avoid the gun, by refusing to rise out of the thick grass, unless very closely pressed.

It frequently happens that a hen florikin, so closely will she squat in the dense grass, is killed by an accidental blow from the stick of one of the beaters; generally at nesting time, for the eggs in the nest (which is made by a mere pressing down of the grass) will often be found close to her hiding place. There are mostly four eggs of a greenish brown colour or olive with spots of dark brown, the eggs are about an inch and a half long, rather pointed at one end like the plover's. The cock bird may be often heard making a croaking kind of noise, though unseen in the high grass; it also, when jumping up, snaps its bill very audibly, and both birds will often utter a sharp screeching note on being flushed. Their food is all kinds of beetles, grasshoppers, and particularly the "blister fly," a diet which even affects their flesh. During part of some seasons it appears that none but brown or hen birds are to be met with, but many of these will be found to be young cocks or cock birds during their yearly change of plumage, for I have shot cock florikin nearly brown all over, except where the black stub feathers were beginning to grow. They fly with their long necks stretched out and equally long legs doubled up under them. The first time I saw a florikin, being then a "howling griffin," it appeared to me like some new kind of duck, though there was no water near, but since then have often shot more of a morning than could be well eaten, for it is hard to leave off shooting them, when they continue rising all round, like trout!

For florikin shooting alone, a long line of horsemen, with a gun carrier between each mounted sportsman, who keep apart, spread out at intervals of two or three hundred yards, is the best plan. An immense stretch of ground can be worked in a morning's ride in this fashion, the person nearest any bird seen, dismounting for the purpose while the beater or gun carrier holds his horse, the rest of the party halt and look on watching the result of the shot. From horseback too a good view over the long grass of distant moving birds can be had.

Shepherds and cattle herdsmen on any small hillocks about will often by waving their waist cloths call the sportsmen to where they have seen florikin jumping up. A very small reward satisfies these willing scouts, while their help will add to the "bag" considerably, for florikin remain much in the same place, so these men, who are out all day, should at least be asked whether they have observed any birds in the neighbourhood. In Malwah, Guzeerat, and Western Kattywar, florikin are very common, but their numbers depend upon good or bad seasons.

Occasionally, but very rarely, the beaters may put up an "houbara," a beautiful bird, a sort of connecting link between the florikin and the bustard. These birds are only to be found in Guzeerat on the Bombay side, but are common enough in Scinde. They frequent very open sandy plains, hiding among any tufts or patches of long dry grass, generally four or five being in company. The "houbara" is about twice the size of a florikin, and has a ruff on the neck of long soft feathers; its back is beautifully mottled, and reminds one of the "tawny" or paler "white owl's" plumage. Their rising and flight too is slow and owl-like. It is a very fine bird in every respect and quite a prize to find. It has the three toes, without any heel or back claw, just the same as the florikin and bustard, so cannot well be mistaken.

The big bird flying overhead in the Plate "1" is the "Indian bustard," a splendid game bird standing quite three feet six inches high and weighing nearly two stone. These grand additions to any "bag" however will not be made while shooting across country with a line of noisy beaters and the constant firing of guns, for they are far too wary to be so easily shot. Unless seen flying overhead about thirty yards high, with the continued easy-going slow flapping of their immense wings, no soaring or gliding *a la* vulture, but with a peculiar flight of its own, impossible to mistake, however far off, the bustard will generally be first discovered by the sportsman while taking his usual scan of the whole country round, through his pocket telescope. A thin white streak will first catch the eye and nothing more: this is the bird's almost swan-like long neck seen above some low grain, cotton, or oil plant field, busily engaged in picking off and snapping at the numerous locusts, grasshoppers, blister flies, &c., &c., to be found at every step, or else the bird itself may be spied stepping very leisurely among low dry bushes and tufts of grass, well out in the open plain, sometimes alone, but often with three or four companions a few paces distant, or again in pairs close together. Now is the time for a chance with the gun, loaded of course with big shot, or better still with Eley's cartridges, though properly speaking bustard shooting belongs to the rifle. First having taken very careful notice of the spot, walk towards it, not in a direct line, but in a careless oblique direction, as if intending to pass wide of the place. It is of no use stooping down or trying on the old idea of walking round the game in an ever-decreasing circle, or any other stalking dodges, for the bird is watching intently your every movement, and would be off at once at the first sign of any such danger signals.

When about one hundred and fifty yards or so off, the bustard, after moving restlessly about a few steps, will begin walking away with its bill pointed high in the air, towards some low bush or the nearest tuft of grass or a big stone even, and there most likely will silently squat down, its head and neck drawn in and whole body hidden by lying as flat as possible. You still walk on most unconcernedly, with only an occasional side glance, and when passing within a hundred yards or less, turn sharp and rush in at best pace, no toddling; this will bring you within fifty yards of the crouching bird, which has meanwhile run out of its hiding place in three or four short skipping bounds with neck and wings stretched out and got on the wing. Now blaze away well forward at the head and neck part, both barrels if necessary, when the game will most likely roll over, a grand flapping heap of feathers, but seldom indeed killed dead. It is as well to keep the second barrel if possible, for often another bustard, hitherto unsuspected and unseen, also rises close by its mate. Frequently I have heard the shot rattle against both body and wings harmlessly enough of this strong close-feathered bird at what ought to have been certain killing range, so always fire at its head, for it otherwise seems shot-proof, unless rising at very close distances, as they sometimes will out of fields of the dense growing oil and cotton plants chiefly, but that chance is a very rare one indeed.

In Khandeish and Guzeerat these birds are very common. I once saw after the rainy season quite fifty bustards rise together out of a very small field, a grand sight, being close to them, while seemingly hiding themselves in some grain. Bustard may be often heard calling, a most curious sound, a sort of booming noise, the note is "oom" "o-o-o-m," very often repeated and long drawn out. It can be heard afar off, and "oom" is one of the names of the bustard in Khandeish. They afford capital marks for rifle practice; there is no need to try and get too close, for if missed from a good distance, the bird will sometimes allow another shot or two to be fired at it before taking the hint and flying off, merely twisting its neck and head suddenly round as the ball whizzes past, but this of course is where they have not been much fired at. In Kattywar I have shot six bustards in about an hour's walk with the "short army Snider Lancaster rifle" at an average of one hundred and fifty yards each, and could possibly have got more, for they were to be seen on all sides on a wide sandy plain. The meat is very good, of a dark brown colour (with a white inside cut on the breast like most game birds), but it is said to be very heating diet like the florikin's flesh. These particular six birds were required for food for a small detachment, or such waste would not have been made all at once.

The natives often contrive to snare the bustard with nooses set for the purpose on the ground they frequent, when these so captured birds are brought round camps for sale, with their eyes closed up by having a feather run through the lids; this is done to keep the bird quiet, and succeeds.

The "Indian bustard" is entirely different from the European one, having a flat black crest on the head, the neck is much longer and white throughout, while the plumage on the back is of a far darker mottled brown colour, the legs and bill being of a light yellow tinge.

The small brown animals seen running at full stretch in the picture are Indian hares. They are about half the size of English ones, and might be mistaken almost for very large rabbits, but that there are no such animals in India. Hares in some places are very numerous, and are to be met with nearly everywhere scattered over the country in open rocky sandy ground, in fields, and chiefly on the banks of rivers where there is plenty of grass cover, as well as in the long patches of shady bushes, broken heaps of rock, boulders and dense tangled jungle generally to be seen in the beds of most dry rivers and big ravines; but they avoid tracts of country where the "bastard teak" tree grows, for the constant rustling of such big leaves would give them no chance against any stealthy foe suddenly pouncing on them asleep. On being started they bolt off much in the manner of rabbits, so require pretty quick snap shooting. They give very good sport coursing with Persian and half-bred English greyhounds, but have a terrible habit of going to earth when at all hard pressed, or rushing for shelter into the middle of some large cactus bush, whence it is almost hopeless to dislodge them. They are very fair eating, making capital soup, but are not to be thought of with their English namesakes in any respect. A dozen or more hares will often fall to the share of each gun in a morning's beat, if the ground has not been too much shot over. They often lie very close and then break back through the line of beaters, so no stragglers should be allowed, or it is impossible to shoot with safety.

The small white animals seen in the foreground are Indian foxes. They are about one third only of the size of an English fox, and are very pretty little creatures of a shiny silver-white colour, with black tip to their brush. They are mostly seen in pairs, a short distance apart on wide open plains, where they are to be met with at every mile or so in the cool mornings. They give famous runs with the aforesaid Persian greyhounds, doubling in the most rapid manner and escaping by sudden turns from the very jaws of the greyhounds. It requires a pair of really good dogs to catch one of these tiny foxes, for during the whole course it looks as if the fox was merely playing with the hounds, and frequently the run ends in the sudden disappearance of the fox in some almost perpendicular hole or hollow between low rocks, for which doubtless it has been making from the first; but very likely this same fox will be met with next morning close to the same place and give just as good a course as before. There is no hunting them by scent, for the heat is too great for any scent to lie, and the whole country is one mass of open earths at very close distances. These little foxes may be heard of an evening and at night barking and answering each other like small lap dogs. Towards the northern part of India there are foxes larger and of a light brown colour.

The small graceful gazelles and the harmless "nil gaiee" or "blue bull" with his does will be mentioned hereafter, for they are not included in sport with fowling pieces. They may be often seen watching the drive with beaters, from a very safe distance, as if quite aware of the fact and so quite unconcerned.

Maj. Gen. W. Rice, Del.

Shaw & Sons, lith

"INDIAN GAZELLE" (CHINKARA). QUAIL SHOOTING.

CHAPTER II.

WILD FOWL SHOOTING.

Snipe Shooting—Teal—Duck Shooting—Various sorts of Duck—Wild Goose Chase.

(*Plate II. shows still further sport with the gun, relating to every kind of Water-fowl to be met with on the splendid "tanks," as Indian lakes are called.*)

First to be considered is the snipe, that most welcome bird, so far ahead of any other small game. How anxiously its arrival is looked for, and with what joy the gunner again sets to work at this never-tiring sport! No sooner has the cold season begun, about November or later, than the snipe also begin to arrive in sufficient numbers to make it worth while getting one's feet wet after them. On first coming in after their long journey from the North they are thin and in poor condition, but after a rest of a week or so recover their flesh and usual swiftness of flight. If sprung during the early morning they rise quite as lively as in England, and with the same delightful note of "s-c-a-p-e!" but if flushed during the heat of the day, are more sluggish, constantly getting up silently, and are much easier to shoot, besides not being so likely to leave any piece of water or marsh they may have settled on during the past night's flight. So this particular sport is generally commenced a little late in the morning when a big "bag" is the object.

For snipe shooting one or two guns are sufficient with a steady beater, or two apiece to pick up and carry the game, spare ammunition, &c., of which latter it is as well to have a good supply, for it is impossible to tell whether the birds may be few or many, fresh arrivals continuing to alight on their passage every night.

The guns are kept well apart, so as not to interfere with each other's shots. Except in "paddy," that is wet green rice fields, and other crops under irrigation, there is seldom room for more than two guns to work side by side, but on any wide marsh or "tank," it is best to keep on opposite sides and slowly beat up and down, driving the snipe backwards and forwards to each other's gun, and so work the ground until the last possible bird is brought to bag. There is little fear of anyone wishing to leave off until this result has been obtained, for it is very hard to think of leaving any behind, although picking up these last few "long bills" is often as hard as making nearly all the rest of the bag, for they get very knowing and wild. It is as well to be prepared for a good ducking at this sport, for one constantly stumbles on some hidden hole, or steps most unexpectedly knee deep in some rotten quagmire, the attention being meanwhile so intently fixed on snipe expected to rise at any moment in any direction.

It is the great variety in the flight or manner of going away of these birds that constitutes the great charm in snipe shooting, for no two shots seem alike; besides one has to keep on the alert more than at any other kind of small game shooting, and though a clean miss of both barrels does sorely hurt one's pride, still a succession of kills is most enjoyable and exhilarating, one comfort too being that longer shots can be taken at snipe than at any other bird, for a single pellet will often cut them over at incredible distances, for they seem very tenderly formed. There are two sorts, one rather smaller than the common snipe, with a pintail, slightly shorter bill, and beautifully marked bars on the end of the wings, but these differences are so slight as to be seldom noticed by sportsmen. These last birds are supposed to arrive from the Straits of Singapore or China.

Later on the little "jack snipe" will be met with, but not in any great numbers. These little "butterflies" lie very close, and there is no fear of their leaving any swamp for a distant marsh, for they mostly pitch again close to where they have been first flushed, so they are generally left to the last to be added to the bag when the "full snipe" have all been accounted for, though these little birds are far better eating even than the big ones. These "jack snipe" mostly get up within a yard or two of one's feet, so very small charges are sufficient to stop their most puzzling flight, generally a zigzag course, high overhead and all round the gunner.

There is another disappointing bird, the "painted snipe," to be met with, when working round lakes and wet rice fields. It is mostly put up where the rushes and reeds are thickest, flying along the top of these in an owl-like manner in a curved course and soon dropping down again. It is not worth powder and shot, though pretty to look at, the hen bird often showing brilliant yellow plumage. From living all the year round in India, it has not the taste of game birds arriving from cooler climes, but the gunner on flushing it almost invariably gets ready as if for its more worthy namesake, so a good deal of abuse falls to this imposter's share.

There is one more very large and rare bird, the "wood snipe." The only one I ever met seemed quite three times the size of a "full snipe." I did not fire, being so much astonished at first, and wishing to get nearer, put up the bird three times, when it flew out of sight, but on each time of rising uttered the exact selfsame "s-c-a-p-e" of the common snipe. This cry first attracted my attention, for till then it seemed like some common sort of wader only. This bird haunted me for a long time, and on comparing notes with a fellow sportsman, found he had met with the same sort of immense snipe at the same place and was equally astonished. This was on a tank in the dense jungle under Champaneer Fort, near Baroda.

Snipe are subject to good and bad seasons, being sometimes comparatively scarce. Twenty or thirty couple are a fair "bag," but fifty will be often made by a good gun, and that bag even it is reported has been frequently doubled, so now the stranger may know what to expect in such a paradise as India certainly is as far as snipe shooting is concerned; undoubtedly the prettiest of all small game shooting. A good silent beater or two, one on either side of the gun, not too wide off, is advisable to recover the birds in passing; of course to run forward to collect fallen snipe, would be the means of scaring away numbers out of shot, so a man with sharp eyes is required to mark well the spot where each bird dropped, for they are often most difficult to find, if only wounded, among tangled weeds and dry grass. I have often tried dogs at this sport, but the fatigue is too much for them and it does not answer, for they splash about and make far too much disturbance.

Snipe shooting should be conducted in a most silent manner, no calling out and at a very slow careful pace, so as not to leave birds behind, for they will lie close enough when the heat is great. Snakes will be met with at this sport, living on the frogs, &c., in the swamps, so better keep a good look out and wear thick boots!

"Teal," precisely like the English ones, begin to arrive directly the "rains" or "monsoon" is over. They are found in small flocks of from twenty to fifty about, generally up winding creeks or deep nullahs full of water, and again on small pieces of water or mere ponds that would be dried up in the hot season. The gunner by creeping up cautiously can often get a close shot that will bring down a dozen or more to both barrels, for they rise up and fly together packed uncommonly close. They will not go far away, and, if not coming round again, which of course gives another chance to the sportsman lying perfectly still and concealed as much as possible, will mostly be found, after flying up and down the creek with extraordinary rapidity and still closely packed, to suddenly wheel round and pitch down under some steep banks. Having well marked the exact spot, creep round alone, and, stooping down very low, run in opposite the very place, when the flock will again rise close enough, and the double shots in their midst can be repeated. Picking up the cripples afterwards is very exciting, for some run ashore trying to hide in grass and bushes, others will keep diving repeatedly; so recovering all the wounded is often a work of time and trouble, in which a good dog is of the greatest assistance, but intelligent beaters will do as well.

Teal, wherever met with, are to be preferred for a shot to duck, being so much better eating, though by far a smaller bird. They get mixed up singly with large flights of duck of all sorts, as they come sweeping down together past the gunner concealed among high flags, rushes, &c., when shooting over any large "tank" or lake, but can be easily picked out, and are not nearly such tough birds to kill as the several ducks.

There is another very good eating teal, the "blue winged" or "Garganey teal," which arrives later on in the cold season, but in vast flocks. These highly prized birds are caught in thousands by the natives every year, and kept for months afterwards in dark "tealeries," low rooms built for the purpose in large European establishments, mostly on the Bengal side or Presidency, affording a delightful change of food long after all wild fowl have left India for cooler climes.

There are still two other so-called "teal"—the little half-white "cotton teal," and the light brown or chestnut coloured "whistling teal." But these birds are found in large numbers on vast sheets of water that are not subject to be dried up during the hot season, and which are covered with vegetation, rank weeds, water lilies, &c. Here they remain nearly all the year round, often quite close to villages and large towns even, for no one molests them, so they become very tame, living in company with moorhens, coots, and such like waterfowl innumerable. These birds are not worth powder and shot, tasting fishy and muddy.

In this same list may be included the large "black-backed goose," or "nukta," so called from the immense protuberance on its bill, quite two inches high, a rounded flat black knob; from this cause also it is called the "comb duck." These birds come in at the end of the rains, and are found on any small open pools of water in batches of six or eight, also in pairs; they are tame, and slow fliers, and it is not quite safe to eat them, for they feed on the wild celery, which is a poisonous plant.

The "ruddy shieldrake," or "Brahminee duck," is also common at the end of the monsoon, and remains for many months longer. It is of a reddish light brown colour, and is a size larger than the biggest mallard. They are sometimes seen about twenty together, or only two or three couples, and again in pairs, standing on the rocky sides of small rivers and bushy ravines. These birds have a peculiar call at intervals of "a-oung," "na-oug," uttered with a nasal twang and not to be mistaken. Nobody ever thinks of shooting or cooking these "Brahminee ducks," for, like the preceding three above named, they are not considered game, and are only here mentioned lest any stranger should wonder what sort of fowl they might be, and so possibly be induced to fire at them by mistake.

We now come to the ducks proper, widgeon and pochards, among which the sportsman may blaze away to his heart's content, for great fun is to be had at these famous birds, both from a shooting point of view as well as for the table, affording as they do such a delightful change of diet to the "toujours mouton," or kid of the previous seven or eight months!

Ducks are well known to be tough and strong on the wing, so full charges of powder and large shot (No. 5 is best) are required to bring them down. They fly at a faster pace too than is their seeming rate of flight, so the golden rule is to always fire forward, aiming at the head and neck part. The birds are often much higher up in the air than appears to be really the case, so some time must be allowed for the shot to reach, for it is of no use hitting them behind; unless struck well forward they do not seem to mind the shot at all, so the keeper's advice to the novice at rabbit shooting should ever be borne in mind, viz., "Shoot where he's going, sir! not where he's been!"

Now, to describe a day's duck shooting. Given a large tank or lake, two or three miles round perhaps, including the usual long creeks leading into it from all sides, the edges covered in most parts with high green reeds, rushes, and flags, also large patches in the more shallow parts of tangled weeds, water lilies, &c., of luxuriant growth. Here let a party of gunners distribute themselves at intervals of a few hundred yards or so apart, well hid among the high reeds and as near the borders of the lake as one can go without getting unnecessarily wet, while perhaps one or two more guns start off in a boat or native canoes to take their chance in the open water. But here let it be said that shooting from a boat somehow does not seem to answer on Indian lakes: the birds are shy of them, and after the first shot or two perhaps give them a wide berth, while the canoes are so crank and ricketty that an upset may be looked for from them sooner or later as almost a certainty. Shooting from a punt with a punt gun I have never seen practised; no doubt terrific hauls and slaughter of wild duck might be made for the first few shots, but most likely the birds being unaccustomed to the sound of such small cannon would depart in a body from that pond for many a day, besides the pleasure of endless individual shots would be lost.

We will suppose that the cold weather season has well set in and that all the ducks have arrived and been settled down steadily feeding for some weeks past on the lake. All the guns being now ready in their several places, with two or three nearly naked beaters, swimmers of course, squatted down well hidden near each sportsman, somebody fires the first shot! when immediately is heard a mighty roar or prolonged rushing sough, a noise difficult to describe, but once heard not to be easily forgotten. This dull deep booming sound is caused by the instantaneous rising of countless thousands of disturbed waterfowl, each towering up for about fifty or a hundred yards high in the air quite straight, then wheeling off round and over the water, circling in large distinct flocks in all contrary directions, alternately lowering and again rising in their course of flight. All seem to be flying at their utmost rate in the wildest state of alarm. The rustling, whistling noise of these innumerable wings is a very pretty sound, almost indescribable. Now is heard from all sides the continued rapid file firing of the hidden gunners, as long streaming flights of duck continue to pass and repass their posts at a sufficiently low course to ensure their being brought down. The falling birds are plainly visible, while great splashes or a sounding bump tells whether each quarry has dropped on land or water. Presently the gun shots begin to be fewer and at longer intervals, while the immense flight of duck have risen meanwhile almost out of sight directly overhead. Numbers in separate bodies are now seen to leave the mass and make off for other distant lakes and pieces of water in the neighbourhood, but soon the chief crowd of waterfowl will begin to descend, still circling round, but in lower and lower flights, being no doubt well tired or affected by the heat of the sun. Again on coming within range they get peppered, and enough can now be shot to make the required "bag," for they are not likely to again rise out of reach, but individuals continue passing to and fro at reasonable distances, while the main body of birds will again settle down on the water, spread out wide all over the surface or trying to hide in the dense weeds and reeds on all sides.

Now begins the work of collecting the fallen, and very troublesome it often proves. Many birds thought to have dropped dead, have recovered and taken to diving and flapping away in the most marvellous manner; but the beaters are quite equal to the occasion, and soon a good pile has been collected to each gun. We will pass over the remarks and discussions of the several sportsmen, as well as their comments on the amount of amusement and quality of the shooting displayed in the day's sport, and proceed while they are refreshing themselves to examine the "bag," among which will be found in greater or less numbers the following varieties of wild fowl, comprising in all ten distinct species, the shortest possible description, for purposes of identification of each different bird, being here given.

First: Our excellent English "mallard" and its mate, both precisely the same as at home and forming the principal part of the bag. Secondly: The "spotted bill duck," one of the very first to arrive in the cold season and the latest to leave. It often stays all the year round, and may be seen with a brood of young ones as early as October. It is a heavy slow-flying bird; they are found in small numbers on tanks where there is plenty of shelter of reeds and rushes. They seem somewhat tame, but will strike one as being the very first ducks of any sort to be met with after the rains. The bill is black with a red spot at the base and yellow at the tip; the legs are very bright red. Both duck and drake are alike and rather larger than the mallard, dirty white colour underneath covered with dark brown spots from breast downwards—good eating. Thirdly: "The gadwall," a smaller duck than the mallard, mottled brown back, with a bright chestnut patch on upper corner of wings, white belly, legs light yellow. Fourthly: "The pintail duck," a beautiful bird; it is easy to recognise from its very peculiar long pointed tail of the two end feathers looking like one or a spike only. Head brown, back beautifully blue mottled, breast white, legs and feet blackish slate brown. The hen bird a little smaller, and its tail not nearly so pointed. It is larger than the mallard and very good eating. It flies with great swiftness and looks very pretty in the sky. Fifthly: "The widgeon," somewhat rare, head and upper part of neck chestnut red with a pale yellow band over the crown, bill of a light blueish lead colour, breast light pink, back mottled grey, tail blackish grey, much white underneath, legs blue lead colour. When flying it makes a very shrill whistling call. It is much smaller than the mallard. Sixthly: "The red crested pochard," another little duck with a most unmistakable red head, the top of which has a yellow crest or band; back, wings, and tail brown, with white patches at both ends of wings; lower part of neck, breast, and belly black, white at the sides; bill, legs, and feet bright red. Hen bird not so brilliantly marked; tip of bill white in both duck and drake. Seventhly: "The red-headed pochard," a smaller bird than the last; head and half the neck chestnut colour, below the neck and breast black, tail also black, beautifully mottled all over back and wings, whiter below; bill blue lead colour with black marks at tip and base; legs and toes lead colour, webs and claws black. Eighthly: "The white-eyed duck," another still smaller pochard than the last, also called "the ferruginous duck," from its iron-red colour nearly all over, except a white bar on the wings and white stomach, bill and legs lead colour or dark slate. Ninthly: "The tufted duck" or "golden eye" of Indian sportsmen, a beautiful dark black duck, with a long silky crest of black feathers; it has a white bar on the wings and white stomach, the rest of the plumage has a green and purple gloss over all, legs and bill lead colour. But it is impossible to mistake either of these birds from the colour of their eyes—they are about the same size. Lastly: "The shoveller," a larger bird than the above, but not nearly so big as the mallard. It can easily be identified by its large broad bill of a dark slate colour, legs red or orange, head and neck greenish brown, breast white, back brown, stomach chestnut, wings light blue and green bars, eye golden. It is a very common duck and stays late on in the season; the female is not of so bright a brown plumage. This duck is not much esteemed, often tasting muddy or rank.

The above-named ten different sorts of duck, with an occasional stranger, will be found to comprise the "bag," affording food enough for a whole camp or station, until another day's duck shooting can be arranged. "Flight shooting" is not practised in India, for there is so much water about that the course of the ducks could not be ascertained with any certainty; still I have done it of a moonlight evening, when encamped close to some good river, but only for the sake of the pot. Relays of duck in small parties pass overhead at a terrific rate, so quite two yards ahead must be allowed for each shot generally. It is as well to send some men down the river waiting at some shallow part or ford to pick up the fallen birds, for they often drop nearly a hundred yards beyond the gun from the impetus of their flight.

Duck shooting at night over tanks or lakes does not answer, for at the first shot almost the birds leave the spot and do not return, the cool night air rendering them lively enough to travel any distance in search of quieter feeding grounds; moreover the shot birds or wounded ones would be hard indeed to retrieve in the dark.

The scene in Plate II. shows the pursuit of wild geese, of which two sorts are to be met with in Central India and Scinde. They are not to be found in the South of India. One is the common wild or "grey lag goose" of England, and precisely similar, with its yellowish red bill and legs. The other is the "pink-footed goose," a smaller bird with a bill dark at the base and tip, but pinkish red in the middle. These birds arrive late in the cold weather in immense flocks of two or three hundred together, and settle down where there are vast lakes with plenty of rushes and reeds on the borders. Unless driven to them by gun shots they seem to avoid smaller pieces of water. All geese are very knowing, and it is difficult to get near them close enough for a shot gun, but they have a habit of huddling up together very closely packed in batches of fifty or more, and trying to hide themselves in clusters of reeds or rushes and weeds that may be growing out some distance from the banks of any large lake. The plan now is to wade in, where possible, behind one of those enormous trusses of cut reeds and flags the natives use for a plank, sitting astride of it and poling themselves along with a long bamboo. These big bundles of long reeds are fastened together round the middle with ropes of twisted grass, and answer the purpose of a boat famously for picking up wounded and dead birds. Such rafts are very unstable and crank, but a ducking from them is little heeded by those using them.

Before starting of course one takes very good care to know that the water is not too deep or mud too sticky, which however is seldom the case, most large pieces of water in India being shallow round the edges, being generally formed merely by the last season's rains, and soon becoming again mere ponds or even quite dry at the approach of the hot weather; then by resting the gun on the truss of reeds and gently pushing it forward, taking good care to keep your

Maj. Gen. W. Rice, Del.t

Shaw & Sons, Lith

A WILD GOOSE CHASE. DUCK SHOOTING

head well down and making no splashing noise, the flock of geese may be reached within about thirty or forty yards. These birds now begin to suspect something, and odd enough collect together in a still closer packed body, with their necks stretched out high up and bills in the air, uttering a low warning note of "hank-hank" to each other in turn. Now silently full cock the gun, depress the bundle of reeds, and blaze both barrels at where the necks seem thickest. The result is like cutting a lane with a scythe through a poppy field almost! Great is the hubbub, loud screaming and calling of the wounded, and those escaping unhurt flying round and over their fallen friends, while in the water a tremendous splashing is going on all around, for birds continue dropping at intervals from above, and those too much hurt to fly are trying to get away at best pace possible with flapping wings; the death flurry too of the dying adds to the disturbance.

Now comes collecting the bag, in which the beaters join eagerly, for they get some of the birds if they like. The one drawback is that these geese will prove so tough that perhaps only one in six will be fit to eat; this tender fit one is discovered by breaking their legs when dead. I have picked up fourteen geese to two barrels loaded with very large shot, in this manner, and most likely as many more birds got away wounded! After being much disturbed by firing, such as a duck shooting party already described would make, the geese which at the first shot have risen to a great height in the air, and there continue flying round and round calling loudly to each other, will begin soon to come down gradually and settle on the lake, as the ducks also do, no doubt feeling the effects of the mid-day sun or getting tired. They now give good shots for a rifle, but somehow few are bagged with ball, for the bullet seems to glance off them.

Geese do a good deal of mischief to crops where they alight

in great numbers. They feed in long rows of fifty or more, each about a yard apart, and walk across a grain field, chiefly "gram," a sort of vetch of which they seem very fond. I have seen three long lines of geese thus feeding of an evening, each row numbering about a hundred birds, and following each other in regular order at about thirty paces interval, so very little of that crop could have been left. Geese fly in long lines while travelling, and sometimes quite low stretched across any river whose course they may be following.

"Bitterns" are often put up out of the long thick rushes on edges of tanks. They are precisely the same as the English birds, and are by many considered good eating, so are added to the "bag." "Herons" of several sorts will also be met with, very numerous in all swampy places, but are never fired at, being said to taste very fishy; but "spoonbills," two or a pair of which are seen flying overhead, are sometimes shot at, being considered by some good eating. A "pelican" is also to be seen on the water; these birds are common on some very large sheets of water and look very grand sailing along, while every now and then they are to be seen with their huge bills up in the air pouching some big fish they have pounced upon. The large nest of weeds with twò long white eggs, each about six inches long, on the ground, belongs to the pair of "sarus" or "dancing cranes," to be seen on the opposite shore. They are fine looking birds quite four feet high or more, with red heads and necks for about four inches down, while their bodies are a pretty French grey or blue. Nobody ever thinks of disturbing them, being very harmless and considered sacred by the natives.

Under the shady tree near the village with its ruined mud fort, may be seen the sportsman's pony with groom, ready to take the "sahib" back to camp with his load of snipe. The powder horn, shot belt, and loading rod speak of days long gone by, but to be remembered still with great delight!

Marvellous indeed have been the changes in fire-arms. The author learnt shooting with a long single-barrel gun of very small bore with a flint lock, but rabbits and even a snipe or two were tumbled to that curious piece of ironmongery, as such a weapon would now-a-days be considered. Should your gun be required to fire ball (round of course), remember to load with not more than a rifle charge, or 2½ drms. of powder for a No. 12 gun, or the excessive kick will spoil all aim at shortest distances even.

CHAPTER III.

BLACK BUCK SHOOTING.

ANTELOPE STALKING—CULLUM, OR CRANES—THE GAZELLE—THE NIL GAI, OR BLUE BULL—A RIFLE REST.

(Plate III. illustrates to the sportsman one of the most pleasing sights in India,—A herd of "Black Buck," as the "Indian-Antelope" are commonly called.)

"BLACK BUCK" are a most graceful kind of deer, and are to be found on nearly all the wide open plains of the Bombay. Presidency, especially where the ground is of a sandy or rocky nature, and where the black soil so favourable for cotton cultivation predominates.

They are to be met with in either small herds of twenty or so, or occasionally in vast numbers of three or four hundred together; but the usual size of a herd is about forty or fifty. Sometimes several herds join together, and then they seem in countless numbers; but this is rare, and appears to take place only once in the year. On the few occasions I have noticed this packing it was just before the rains set in.

A small herd of about twenty deer will always have one fine black buck as leader and master, with perhaps a younger one or two, either just turning black, or of a rich chestnut colour. The rest are does and fawns in all stages of growth; but it is only the very young kids that are to be remarked as such, for the rest soon run up to the average size and height, so as not to be easily distinguished from the older full-grown does.

A very fine old black buck would stand about two feet nine inches high, but they vary a good deal according to locality in size as well as in the length and spread of their horns. The does are rather smaller, of a light fawn colour, with a pale yellow streak along the flanks, white underneath the belly and inside the legs. The quite young kids are of a darker red fawn colour, with softer or more fluffy hair. Nobody ever touches these, or the pretty gentle does either, unless perhaps a single one that may be required for the beaters or hunters' pot when very hard up for meat, so the black buck alone will be discussed.

As an excuse for shooting him, let it be stated that black buck are very good eating, and the older the better in taste; many people seem to think contrary to the general opinion regarding a rank old goat. The meat is of a dark brown colour, and very close grained, with hardly any fat—altogether excellent. The next excuse is the splendid target practice he affords, with a fine pair of horns for the prize of superior marksmanship. There can be no better test of good shooting than knocking over a buck at any of the extraordinary ranges he presents himself to be fired at, when it is remembered that the rifleman must not only form the most accurate idea or judgment of any given distance, at a very short notice too, but be able to find himself steady enough, after perhaps a very long tramp over ploughed fields and broken undulating stony ground, to properly aim or cover the object, so as to ensure hearing without fail that delightful "thud," or dull flop sound that follows the successful shot.

Bucks can be approached sometimes, but not often, within one hundred yards, but then they are sure to be restless, and if not moving off or racing by in their course, will seldom allow a steady shot to be taken. This is always supposing that no such means or dodges as riding up to them in a bullock cart, or walking behind a led cow are resorted to, for by many such methods they can often be shot at quite close, but the deer soon learn to avoid such suspicious looking traps, so the ruse has to be tried on at far distant and ever-changing localities. Besides, there is little sport when the deer are so outmanœuvred, for killing becomes then almost a certainty.

These plans are mostly put in practice by beginners at buck shooting, or those gunners who have not much confidence in their skill with the rifle. Walking past in an oblique direction, talking meanwhile quite loudly with a beater on the near side, who may carry or not a few green twigs on his head to represent a burden, will often bring you within reasonable distance of the deer. Of course you must both walk most unconcernedly, as mere travellers, and looking as if the herd were not even known to be there—no stooping down or attempting any kind of stalking tricks, for the whole lot of antelope, though seemingly intent only on grazing, are watching narrowly your every movement. Having got a little way beyond, as if merely continuing your journey, and still talking, the deer will become less suspicious. You can now venture to slacken your previous rather slow pace, and turn round, letting the beater still walk on alone, when the buck, who has never left off staring at you, will most likely stand still long enough for aim to be taken at what may be a sure killing distance, according to your skill in the use of the rifle. Had you attempted in the first instance to walk up within range, then stop short, and, perhaps, kneel down to fire, the buck would just have started off at a run, and taken very good care indeed that day never to let you come again within the same reach by a long way, for they are very knowing animals after being fired at, as no doubt has been repeatedly the case with every black buck within many miles of any cantonment or station.

The modern "express rifle" and low trajectory of the "Martini-Henry," and other rifles, must make buck shooting almost a certainty, but the deer have doubtless long ago learnt to keep the hunter at a still greater distance, so the sport should be as good as ever.

We will now suppose that the sportsman has, on reaching his ground, taken a good look round through his small pocket telescope as usual, so as to be able to decide which particular buck to go after, the blackest in sight, and by consequence the best pair of horns being of course selected. There are exceptions to this rule, but it is a pretty general one to follow, the bucks getting blacker in their coats as they grow older, and their horns increasing in length with age also. Perhaps the glass will have shown, just over some distant ridge or undulating ground, merely the tips of a pair of wide horns, looking like two black sticks set upright, nothing else being visible. This will be a fine black buck lying down chewing the cud, as they do for hours, chiefly during the middle of the day. Now is a grand chance for the hunter to put in practice all his stalking notions; taking good care, of course, to keep well to windward, and starting alone, it will be his own fault only if he does not manage to get very close indeed.

If necessary to see more of the game, having the rifle quite ready, and being meanwhile well breathed or steady, a low whistle will cause the buck to start up, and while it is staring around for a very few seconds, give time for a shot, which will roll him over for good, after a frantic jump or two in the air, head well up; or else the chance of getting near enough to the herd, as shown in the plate, may be preferred.

Here the country is open as possible, for the antelope, being often a good deal bothered by wolves, and even jackals, looking after their fawns, which they have to leave behind, lying hid among low tufts of grass or stunted bushes, on being themselves driven away by any sudden scare, take good care to select some spot where a clear view all round can be taken of any coming foe, and where, while some keep watch, the rest of the herd can repose in safety.

The hunter now begins his careless stroll towards the deer, taking particular pains that his rifle shall be kept out of view. This is best done by slinging it, stock downwards, on, but not across, the right shoulder, barrel behind, so as not to project in any way, while the right hand lightly clasps the sling in front, so as to prevent the rifle slipping off the shoulder. Carried in this manner the heaviest rifle will feel quite light, can be instantly brought to the "ready," and the fingers do not feel numbed, as is often the case after grasping a heavy weapon for miles, and all glitter from the barrels is avoided, which is the cause of more lost shots than most people imagine. By the time the gunner has got within about three hundred yards or so, the wary does, always the first to take alarm, begin, after a prolonged stare, to wheel round slowly and walk restlessly about, pretending to graze for a moment or two, and then looking up again for another stare; this soon ends in one doe springing forward a few steps, while the rest break into a short trot for a few paces, ending in a succession of high-bounding leaps, each seeming to vie with one another which can leap highest. Nothing can be prettier than this sight of a large herd all jumping and spread out in a long string or drove. Perhaps it is performed to gain a clearer view on all sides, so as not to run heedlessly into the aforesaid wolves' clutches, or other dangers, for, after going about a hundred yards or more they will as suddenly stop leaping, and remain standing still in a group, but looking well all round.

Before this short stampede of the whole herd has begun, some younger, blackish brown-coloured bucks have most probably been engaged in a tilting match in the midst or just outside the rest of the does grouped about. These contests seem to be incessantly going on all day, and are, no doubt, trials of strength and pluck. The bucks begin by standing a few yards apart in front of each other, horns well

Maj. Gen. W. Rice, Delt. Shaw & Sons, Lith.

A HERD OF "BLACK BUCK" OR "INDIAN ANTELOPE".

lowered, and after a little dodging in circles and stamping of the fore feet, they suddenly rush or jump forward in the manner of goats, butting one another. Now follows a long struggle, horns interlaced, and foreheads almost touching, alternately pushing one another a few paces backwards. Each round seems to last quite five minutes, when they suddenly leave off, look about a little, and begin the struggle again. The younger red bucks, though often having fine-grown, long horns, never seem to indulge in these bouts, but look on attentively at them with the does.

All this time the stately old lord of the herd has been either slowly stalking among the does, occasionally giving one of them a vicious and seemingly unnecessary poke with his horns behind, which sends her forward with a jerk, perhaps uttering at intervals a short grunting sort of bark (from which sound by the way his native name of "boorka," or old goat, is derived), or else, suspecting danger, he has been staring hard at the coming enemy. At any rate he, their leader, will be the last to fly, always moving after the now retreating herd in a stately manner, and, with no unnecessary haste, bringing up the rear. It is best not to wait for this last move, but take him while standing still, and affording a fair shot. Never mind about a little extra distance. You have only to run up the slide, or sights, a longer "range" than you believe requisite, by from fifty to a hundred yards, then taking a "very fine sight," aim at the lowest part of the buck's stomach, seeing the whole of his body clear above the "fore-sight," thus giving quite fifteen inches for any miscalculation of distance. The ball cannot fall short under these circumstances, and has still less chance of going over or high, for deer are sure to be farther off than they seem by a few yards, more or less, so the bullet reaches its mark fairly somewhere in the buck's depth of body or side, either at once dropping him on his back, with much sprawling and kicking out of legs in the air, or else with a forward jerk and stagger he tries to catch up the herd, already racing off full stretch at the sound of the shot, or runs round in a short circle, and falls flat, dead, or else quietly pretends he has not been hit at all, and begins to nibble grass, looking up as if quite unconcerned at every few steps. No other animal can so cleverly act this part; but against this strange, puzzling behaviour, you have the welcome "thud" or flop sound to count on. No hurry is now needed; slip in a fresh cartridge, take a long, satisfying view of him through the telescope, and wait a few minutes. The buck will soon lie down, when you can walk up and settle him, calling up two or more beaters from the distance by a waive of your hat or handkerchief. These men come running up, pleased enough, for they get the paunch, &c., as their share; this they squeeze out previous to hoisting the deer on a short bamboo pole or thick stick, cut for the purpose close by, and so carry off the venison slung on their shoulders between them to the nearest village. The weapon used in this case has been the "short Snider army rifle oval bore, ·577," than which nothing can be better for the purpose.

Often a solitary old buck, expelled the herd by younger and stronger rivals, will be met with; he is sure to be worth a shot, but is, perhaps, restless, and much inclined to bolt, even when too far off to make sure of. Now, just give a sharp, shrill blow or two on the "railway whistle" (the best sort the hunter can carry, either for signalling beaters or stopping game at speed); the buck, on hearing this noise, will pull up sharp, and wheel round to stare at you, showing no flank view; but this is just the best possible sort of shot, for no rifleman ever shoots wide, though the bullet may go over or fall short. Put up almost any probable range or "sight," and fire at the buck's feet. One of three things will happen—he either gets his throat cut, or is raked clean through, or there is "a row in his timber yard," in cricketers' parlance, meaning one or more broken legs to limp off on. Not but that a deer, with one leg only broken, either fore or hindmost, will manage to run nearly as well as if untouched; for I have known many a long run after one so lightly wounded; though well mounted, the deer would keep just in front of the horse's nose for three or four miles even, and then most suddenly drop, panting, and so utterly done up that it could be handled and have its throat cut. This last operation requires care, or a prod with the horns, or ugly kicks from the hoofs will follow.

All the above common incidents in antelope shooting are detailed for the information of novices only. The plan I prefer for roaming over a country, as well as for bringing home the game, is to be mounted on a good riding camel (as shown in the plate). Both gun and rifle can be taken with you, besides a beer bottle, &c., most acceptable after, perhaps, a thirty mile ride or more, in any direction or circuit. You are then ready for snipe, duck, florikin, or whatever may show itself in the shape of game. The camel used constantly to return home laden, and looking like a poulterer's shop, with, perhaps, one or two black buck, a gazelle, bustard or two, several florikin, ducks, snipe, hares, and, perhaps, some "koolung," or "cullum," as they are commonly called, hanging down on both sides. This last-named bird is the pretty blue "demoiselle crane," a flight of which appear just beyond the small tank, with its embankment of mud—the "bund," so common everywhere for damming up any small piece of water in India. Flocks of several hundreds of these handsome birds are often to be seen circling round and round, almost out of sight, but still distinctly audible, for their call, "kar-kurra," "kar-kurra," repeated without ceasing, is so clear, that it can frequently be heard when the flock are still invisible in the brightest sky. They fly in a wedge shape, also in lines of great length, and half circles; and before alighting soar round and round, calling to each other. They are very good eating, so well worth powder and shot; but it is very difficult to get near enough to a flock with the gun, for they post sentries, who give the alarm, and off goes the whole body, screaming. A rifle bullet sent into the "blue," or where they are standing thickest packed together, will often cut over two or three.

These birds stand about three feet high, and are very handsome, the plumage being much esteemed for ladies' hats; general tint, a French grey. They appear most regularly in the cold season, just as the corn fields are cleared of their crops. This punctuality is referred to in Scripture. They seem fond of water, keeping near rivers, but do not wade. Of these birds there are two sorts, one far smaller than the other, called "grus virgo," while the larger, "grus cinerea," has the plumes so much in request.

Sometimes a herd of antelope will be seen to consist of does and fawns alone; but soon the buck will be found in company of a single doe, about a quarter of a mile from the rest of the herd; they are merely courting, so like to be alone. Should the master of the herd be shot, another takes his place directly, arriving from some direction miles away in some cases; for there must be a leader, or follower rather, to every herd, for whenever the deer move off, the buck will be found bringing up the rear, and never, or rarely indeed, in front.

The black buck horns are much prized, making capital hat pegs or ornaments for walls; the skins also make pretty mats. I once shot a pair of horns, twenty-seven inches long from tip to base in a straight line, and have seen another pair still longer, which, oddly enough, belonged to a young red black buck; these last horns were almost smooth, and very slightly twisted, growing almost parallel, a very unusual occurrence.

The wider apart horns spread, and the more marked the rings on them appear, and the greater the twists or curves, the better they look. The horns are never shed or dropped; but a few days after being shot they will easily untwist from the skull, when a rubbing with sand and oil greatly improves their appearance.

Where plentiful, I have shot six fine black buck in a morning's walk, and could have exceeded this number even, had so much meat been required.

On the bare, open plain this would have been difficult, for the herds race out of sight on hearing a distant shot; but black buck, at times, frequent places where there is much high, dry grass and stunted bushes about, when, seeming to trust in such cover, they are not so shy, and a shot can be had at every half mile or so. On these occasions they mostly seem to have left the herds, for the does and fawns are not found with them in numbers as usual.

The big bird on the right in the picture is a bustard. Two villages, with their mud or stone forts, are in the distance; also another large herd of antelope.

The "Indian gazelle," mentioned above, and shown in Plate I., is a very pretty little kind of deer, standing about two feet two or three inches high, of a dark red chestnut colour, with curved horns, of quite a foot long, the lower half of which are set with rings, the upper part plain, with very sharp points. The does also of this most graceful little deer have horns, but mere thin, limp, smooth apologies, about six inches long, evidently not intended for defence or fighting purposes, like the bucks.

The common name for the gazelle is "chinkara," also "kal-sipi;" this last, from its little black tail, which is incessantly on the move, and often helps to attract the attention of the cautiously peering hunter. They are found out in the open plains, and on low, undulating ground; also among low scrub bushes, but not in great numbers together, mostly one buck with two or three does in company. They are very common; and these small family parties will be met at every half mile or so, in likely places.

On some sandy plains, with patches of low thorn bushes here and there, these little deer may be seen scattered in parties of two or three, with an occasional single buck, all around. On such ground a rare bag may be made among them, but of course a good deal of walking is required, for a shot sends them bounding and scampering off in all directions, but they soon pull up again.

This deer shooting is very pretty rifle practice, for the mark is only about a foot wide, but they can be approached much nearer than the black buck. On seeing the hunter the small party of gazelles will run off, dodging round and over the low scrub bushes, the little buck last of all, at a high-actioned, stately, long trot. Now either blow the whistle, or imitate at intervals the peculiar loud sneeze or snorting sound these goat-like little deer indulge in, and from which their native name of the "sneezer" is derived. This noise will at once cause the buck to wheel round sharp and stand still fronting you, looking eagerly about all round, for he takes the sound for the challenge of a rival buck, and stands, stamping his fore feet indignantly. All this gives time to bring the rifle to bear on his chest, or, perhaps, neck only, for they mostly contrive to look over some obstacle, showing as little of the rest of their body as possible, when a quick shot will drop the small buck. There must be no delay in firing, for the game does not wait still long, but is off to follow the more timid retreating does, again and again wheeling round to satisfy his curiosity at farther distances.

These small bucks may be often seen fighting in a most determined manner, butting at one another, and, with horns locked together, each striving to push his opponent backwards or over. It is easy to get near two bucks thus engaged for a close shot. The fawns are very pretty, almost woolly little creatures, with immense black, soft eyes. They are sometimes found in tufts of grass and bushes, where they have been left hidden by the does. These fawns can be easily tamed; but they become dangerous pets, for they take to butting every thing and body as soon as their horns are grown. The meat of these small deer is excellent venison. It is of little use slipping greyhounds at gazelles, or antelopes either, both being far too fleet; one "kill" would not fall to a hundred runs or courses.

The "nil-gai," also shown in Plate I., commonly called the "blue bull," is the largest of the Indian antelopes, standing, with its head up, nearly six feet high, but only about four-and-a-half at the shoulder. It has short, blunt horns, pointing nearly upright, about nine inches long. The bulls alone have horns, and the old ones are of a dark blue slate colour, while the does and young ones are of a light reddish brown. This big beast is not much thought of by sportsmen, for, though its meat is good, nobody wants so much in the larder at once. Natives, as a rule, will not touch it, stupidly believing the animal to be a sort of cow, and consequently sacred; this too in spite of the does having no horns, and other signs besides, showing its resemblance to large deer. "Nil-gai," as they are termed, collectively, are found in small herds of from six to twenty or more. In Western Kattywar I have seen quite one hundred together, no doubt many small batches having joined to make up so large a drove. They then frequented a vast open sandy plain, where much salt was left by the receding sea at certain times of the year.

Occasionally, a very big black-looking solitary bull is to be met with; such a one will give a famous run on horseback, going very fast, at an easy long stride or canter, clearing high cactus bushes and wide fences with a bound, and taking the wide nullahs or watercourses without an effort seemingly, so it is quite a feat to spear a large bull. Generally speaking no one ever molests them, so they become very tame, doing much damage to grain crops, which they invade at dusk; but if a bull is shot, the natives will often beg the skin to make shields, from the immensely thick, tough leather part round the neck; this skin is nailed down on boards till dry, then highly varnished, and shaped with much taste. A common name for this antelope is "roz," applied to both sexes alike. They are mostly met with in low thorn-bush jungles, and on the outskirts of forests; and sometimes by very young sportsmen or new hands have been mistaken for the "samber," or does of the largest Indian stag (elk); but a glance at the heels or feet of these "nil-gai" will show the very conspicuous white rings round their fetlocks, a most distinguishing mark.

Once, while marching, an artillery friend begged a shot with my Snider rifle at a big bull, lying down six hundred yards off on some white, salt, sandy plain; the bull turned over, with its legs stuck up rigidly in the air. On our going up, one eye was found hanging out, having been so punched out by the ball entering the other eye; this shot literally scoring "a bull's eye!" The beef was hoisted on to a gun limber, and feasted the detachment. This animal is supposed to be the "hippelaphus" of Aristotle, or "horned horse" of the showman.

Apropos of long shots, the following hints will be found useful for using

"THE VERY BEST RIFLE REST!"

For long shots at black buck, or other deer, the sportsman will find that these knowing animals will seldom allow him to take a kneeling shot at them, starting off at a run directly they see any such preparations for their destruction, in the most provoking manner, so the best plan in these cases is to use the rifle sling, by which quite as good shooting can be made in the "standing position" up to four hundred yards or more, as in any "kneeling position" whatever; to say nothing of the time saved for a shot at an already alarmed buck disposed to run off, or the bother of getting down to the cramped kneeling position, when the game is often then found to be completely hidden by high grass or intervening bushes, &c. The left arm held out straight is passed through until on or just beyond the elbow joint, the very loose pendent sling (which must be regulated by the sliding buckle to each rifleman's proper length of arm). The left hand held open—knuckles downwards—is then again passed over and under the sling, when it grasps the stock about a foot beyond the trigger guard. A double twist of the sling is thus obtained, which on the rifle being brought up to the "present" will be found to afford a most steady firm rest, the left elbow being drawn down by the sling nearly under the barrel. Thus used the sling gives such support that the rifle might be held at the "present" for ten minutes, with less fatigue than by the ordinary system for a minute. The right hand is still at liberty if necessary to alter the slide of the "back-sights" for any moving off object to any "distance."

To begin this movement the rifle should be held by the right hand on a level with the breast, muzzle rather raised, when the left arm can be easier passed through the pendent sling. Of course the lower end of the sling is fastened to within four inches or so of the butt or heel plate, as in all sporting rifles, and not in the useless stupid plan of just before the guard as seen in some old regulation arms. This dodge was shown me nearly forty years ago, but by whom I have quite forgotten. I have never seen it done by any one else. It is soon acquired by a very little practice indoors, and will afterwards never be discontinued. It is not generally known, or would not be here mentioned. The shooting of troops by its means would be increased threefold at any distances, and save infinite trouble with recruits or beginners. No recoil is felt when thus using the sling, for it presses the butt well home to the shoulder when at the "present," and prevents the rifle jerking up or throwing high, if loosely held, on being fired. The now open formation of troops permits of this "sling rest" being easily used. The support it gives while waiting for a shot with a heavy sporting rifle is something delightful; the right arm can be dropped altogether if preferred until it is needed to the very moment for bringing up the rifle to the "present." Sometimes the hunter will find he has to wait in expectation of a shot at game passing some small open space at any instant, when, from so long waiting at the "ready," his arms feel quite tired out and very unsteady; only let him seek relief by this plan, when long waiting becomes of little account. To all riflemen I would say "*experto crede*," and, but that it sounds so like boasting, I can declare by means of this rest alone to having cut over, at standing shots with the 400 yards sight up, black buck by the dozen.

When walking towards deer, the method already described of carrying the rifle hung by its sling on the right shoulder is also strongly recommended (it can be shifted to the left shoulder of course for ease at times). The right hand on the sling in front prevents the sling slipping off the shoulder, while it can be readily prepared for the "sling rest," just described, by the hunter, as he continues his slowly advancing pace, slipping his left arm through the sling, slightly lowering and turning the muzzle towards the deer in so doing, they will then first be made aware of the rifle's presence by its report and smoke; whereas by carrying the rifle in any other way the watchful deer are too often scared by a full view of the protruding gun barrel, flashing as it does on any change in carrying the weapon like a waving sword in the bright sunlight, enough to cause a stampede for miles of every herd in view! A rifle carried thus is harmless in case of accident from a fall, stumble, &c.; the ball merely goes to heaven, instead of perhaps sending some one there!

Before starting for a walk across any herd of deer, it is as well to take a good view through the small telescope (of course avoiding as much as possible any flashing from that generally shining object), in the direction one is likely to fire, for cultivators are often engaged in their fields far beyond, and while stooping or sitting down over their work, are perhaps quite out of sight. It is very unpleasant to hear the yells these people naturally make on a rifle ball whistling and "ricocheting" over their heads, as with the present long-range weapons will sometimes occur, unless great care is taken.

While on the subject of guns, those who have not been in the habit of firing very large charges with very heavy fire-arms had better first try a shot or two at a very small mark, such as a wafer stuck on a wide tree stump at about eighteen inches from the ground, and at about eighteen paces distant (the average height of most dangerous animals' heads, and distance of most shots obtained in thick jungle). The novice will probably find himself knocked off his balance, and the ball will have struck about a foot or more above the mark aimed at, while it will be some time before he is prepared to put in the second barrel or shot.

Should the small piece of ordnance here described be entrusted to any native to carry, the sportsman may rest assured it will not be forthcoming in time on an emergency! The experience thus gained may save the beginner from a miss or some accident with the first wild beast he attempts to shoot. The golden rule of all is "never to part with your rifle" for an instant, for the chances are directly it is out of your hand some grand and most unexpected shot will offer itself and be lost, to the intense chagrin of all concerned. If too weak or lazy to be troubled with what seems a cumbersome rifle, better stop at home and leave the work for manlier hands, for being caught unarmed is the source of very many so-called accidents.

CHAPTER IV.

HOG HUNTING.

DESCRIPTION OF WILD BOAR—KHUBBER, OR NEWS—PRELIMINARY ARRANGEMENTS—THE BURST—THE RUN—SPEAR AND KILL—DETAILS—ARAB HORSES—TUSKS AS TROPHIES—BEATING TACTICS—AN OLD 'UN—DOGS BAITING HOG—DOUBTFUL PORK.

(Plate IV. illustrates what is universally admitted to be the finest sport in all India, viz., Hog Hunting, commonly called "Pig-sticking!")

FIRST, to describe the "Indian wild boar." A full-grown boar will stand over two feet and a half, and from snout to end of tail will be quite six feet. His colour is a very dark brown, almost black, with a grand thick row of very stout long black bristles, planted from the top of the head right along the back, an extra thick bunch of nearly upright bristles showing about a foot from where the tail begins. He has a very splendid pair of most coarse back-flowing black whiskers, as thick as wire. These whiskers turn grey with age, but are far from then giving a mild venerable appearance to their owner; the ears are pointed and stuck round with long bristles; his lower tusks are beautifully white and gleaming, while the short, thick, much-curved upper ones are yellow and dirty looking; the tail is quite straight, no curling and almost bare, but has a flat tuft of bristles sticking out on either side at its end; the fore legs are covered down to the knee with just such long, thick, backwards-curving bristles as the whiskers, and like them turn grey with age. The sow is more lady-like in appearance, of a lighter brown colour, without the tusks, and whiskers not so pronounced; general form slighter altogether in build. The "squeakers" are also brown and light in shape. The very little ones are of a light grey colour with several dark reddish-brown stripes in rows along their flanks lengthways.

These wild pigs live in herds or "sounders," as the sporting term is, of from ten to sixty or more, while two or three boars or a fine solitary old fellow are found sometimes lying up in separate adjacent bushes by themselves, far from the rest of the family. They choose most unexpected places, such as under small haystacks, in thick garden hedges, in single dry cactus and thorn bushes, in rocky caves, in date groves and patches of cover, in the beds of dry rivers, and under self-made heaps of dry cut reeds and long grass, &c. The mischief these animals cause to both ripe and unripe crops is very great, travelling as they do for the purpose from astonishing distances, feeding all night and setting off back again for their fastnesses in some hill or dense jungle a little before dawn. This plan is repeated nightly as long as there are crops worth visiting. They are not to be turned from their course homewards in a hurry on these occasions, for I have twice seen a large "sounder" so travelling, rush through the ranks of an infantry and also cavalry regiment on the line of march, just at daybreak, making good their retreat without loss, but causing much surprise and confusion.

This chance of meeting or intercepting a "sounder," however, cannot be reckoned upon, for their next night's foraging expedition might be in another direction altogether. The big boars lead the herd or drove in these cases, the sows and young ones are in the middle, and a few big boars bring up the rear, all keeping in a pretty compact body go straight ahead as described across country. Should the hog decide to stop for the day or longer in some likely cover affording plenty of food and shelter, such as high corn or a cane field, the fact is soon discovered by the men employed all night long on high stands in the middle of the fields, watching their crops to try and drive off such destructive animals as "nil-gai" deer, pigs, and even bears at times, bent on visiting them.

Now comes the hunter's turn. The news or "khubber," as the well-known welcome word is called, is sent off sharp by some quick runner, or if too far, is so passed on from village to village until it reaches the camp or station. Now a scene of excitement prevails: as many sportsmen as can be collected or spared from their duties hastily start off their best hunters with spears, &c., in charge of their respective grooms, while they themselves follow shortly after at a canter together. On arriving at the place where the "sounder" has taken up its quarters, the ground is found to be surrounded or "ringed" by men up trees and other high places, on the watch to prevent the swine slipping away unobserved. A large party of beaters have been meanwhile collected from the neighbourhood under the guidance of some well-qualified leader, and are awaiting the arrival of the huntsmen. Now a consultation is held as to the probable number of hogs in cover, the best line of country to drive them out on, and proper directions are given to the mass of beaters to act in concert. A few scouts are sent out and placed up distant trees with small flags or little bits of white cloth tied to a long bamboo to point out the direction of any retreating big boars; for these cunning old rogues having probably been in many such hunts since their infancy, have perhaps got an idea of what is going on, and will often try to slink off unobserved before the cover is beaten; a neighing horse or the stamping of their hoofs, or any calling out near their lurking place, is quite sufficient to cause such knowing old hogs to slip away quietly by themselves; so too much silence in the making of all preliminary arrangements cannot be insisted upon.

The "captain of the hunt" now tells off his party in twos, mostly settled by "drawing lots," or otherwise at the last minute, and directs them where to take up their places on different sides of the cover, of course leaving the points from which the pig are expected to break perfectly open. The beaters with small drums, match-locks to fire blank charges, and all armed with stout sticks, stones to throw in likely corners, the spare spears or any handy weapons, are ranged in line as closely as possible. The word is given, and instantly a deafening row begins as all advance at a very slow pace. The shouts, drums, and guns awake the swine, who begin hustling about in the cover, making short runs to and fro, for they fear to break at once into the open plain. Meanwhile, the horses, well knowing what is coming, are in the wildest state of excitement, quivering all over, pawing the ground and boring at their bits. Soon the men nearest the cover shout the announcement that first one big boar and then another has taken to the open! Still all the nags must keep their places, for if not allowed to get away a reasonable distance, or what he considers a fair start, the hog would, if pursued, instantly dash back into the cover, from which it would be next to hopeless to again dislodge him, for he would take up his post in the densest part, and charge again and again everybody that came near him!

But say a proper start has been signalled from the farthest trees, the order to "go" is given to the first couple of horsemen, and off they fly, best pace, for now comes the all-exciting race for "first spear," or the boar's nine-inch tusks for the prize to the rider who first draws blood. They soon draw near the boar, who on hearing the clatter of hoofs behind him at once puts on extra speed; there is no need to call upon the horses to follow this example, for they are already doing their best most willingly. About a quarter of a mile or more brings them up within twenty yards or so of the pig,

Maj. Gen. W. Rice, Delt. Shaw & Sons, Lith

HOG HUNTING. DRIVING A 'SOUNDER' OUT OF SUGAR CANE.

who at once begins to change his late slightly diverging course for a very straight one indeed. Each hunter now strives, though keeping his horse well in hand, to secure a good lay in, riding close side by side, and partly lengthening their spears, keeping the now pressed boar as straight before them as possible, like a couple of greyhounds with a coursed hare before them, each ready to take advantage of the slightest swerve on the pig's part to either side, to put on the needful spurt and prod him in passing. It is anybody's race, for as the twenty yards are lessened to five only, a succession of sharp loud angry snorts announce the now nearly blown hog's indignation with the whole performance; glancing hastily to either side he begins to slightly falter in his course—the lucky moment has arrived, the faintest possible touch of the spur, most likely insensibly given, sends one brave steed past with a lightning rush, the spear point is lowered and in the next half second buried deep with the mere impetus of the pace, in the boar's flank. "Spear!" is called to the companion horseman, equally close pressing on the pig, and who is also ready to take his turn at the hog, as it, swerving from the late thrust of steel, crosses his front, when a fresh wound is scored.

The boar, not at all relishing these so quickly following digs in the ribs, snorts most angrily and swings round in earnest, trying hard to rip the last passing horse, with a most vicious leap high up at the nag's chest or flanks, accompanied with a chorus of loud most startling grunts, but as this revengeful move has been half expected by both the well-trained horse and his rider, so it is avoided by a wheel outwards to the left just in time, the hint being given and as instantly obeyed at the lightest touch of the bit.

The hog now begins to waddle slowly forward, bleeding and foaming at the mouth and quite ready for a most rapid wheel round and vicious charge, all his bristles well erect, as first one horseman and then the other overhauls him, and soon either kills him dead with a deep thrust under or behind rather the fore-arm, or has a spear-head snapped off short by mere muscular force of the pig, or the spear is dragged out of hand and so left sticking in the hog's back. This loose spear, swaying from side to side at every step, soon pulls up the boar, when first staggering, then sitting up on his haunches, with mighty sighs he presently rolls over dead, without a single groan or cry to betray his agony or fear of death! Now jump off your panting snorting nags, turn round their heads to what breeze there may be, loosen their girths, and beckon the fast-running beater or two who with spare spears have followed the late run at incredible speed. While the thoroughly blown horses are being led to and fro by their owners, a few details connected with the art of "pig-sticking" can be explained.

The spears used on the Bombay side or Presidency have light steel heads and sockets; those lance-shaped are best, for they cannot stick in the boar's ribs as will sometimes happen. The stout male bamboo, not a hollow one, is as long as the hunter on foot can reach high with his open hand (longer would be not only heavy to wield, but difficult to carry), so as not to be caught or knocked out of hand when diving under and through dense thorn bushes, past low branching trees, &c., as will often happen in a run. There is no weight or balance of lead at the spear's foot, for it is not wanted, the point never being lowered until the last moment or so required for use; at other times it is held grasped about the middle, close to the horse's right flank, the point projecting about a foot only above the nag's ears and rather across his neck high up. Total length of spear seven and a half to eight feet at most, with leather covers over the blades to protect them from rust, &c., when not in use. Many serious accidents occur from incautiously holding spears, both on horseback and off, so great care should be taken that they are properly carried at all times. It is as easy to detect a novice at "pig sticking" from neglect of these most essential precautions, as a duffer at billiards or dangerous shooter from his method of handling a cue or gun.

The horses best suited for the sport are Arab stallions (mares are never ridden in Western India); other horses would not have the courage to face a grunting boar, for the short, deep, loud "wough, wough!" he utters on being roused and while charging, is very nearly as startling as a tiger's roar on being hit with a bullet, and very similar in sound. These Arab hunters are small, rarely over fourteen and a half hands, and if even smaller by an inch or so are none the worse, for they seem then to be more clever on their feet, avoiding deep sudden holes and fissures in the ground, quite invisible until you are right over them; skipping over broken piles of rock, avoiding tree stumps, dropping into ravines and scrambling up the opposite banks, pounding down rocky hill sides, altogether behaving in a most cat-like manner, and getting clear over broken ground where a big horse would knock himself to pieces and be nowhere in the run. They are quite up to twelve stone as a rule and can clear nullahs surprisingly, though they mostly fail at any high leaping, but of this luckily there is little or none, beyond an occasional mud wall seldom over two and a half feet high and slightly built at top; hedges round fields can always be crashed through, for they are never staked or firmly bound.

The theory or axiom of hog hunting is "that where a pig can go a horse can follow," but it is very often a puzzler, for the boar, knowing every inch of the ground from his earliest days, of course selects the very worst possible line of country in his flight, in the hope of shaking off his pursuers, and very often succeeds in so doing, for his cunning dodges are numerous indeed. A clever little Arab hunter that knows his work from practice takes quite as much delight in the sport as his rider, and will often seem to kill the boar single handed, sticking close to his tail and following every turn and double without any help from the bridle. Scattered patches of thick thorn bush jungle will be met with in most runs; here the hog by suddenly pulling up sharp and lying down when passing any particulary thick bush, will often throw the sportsmen completely out, and while they have gone ahead some distance before missing him, he has doubled back and got clear off in any other direction. The two riders keeping a little wide of the boar and close behind him must see him carefully through all these obstacles, of course at a slower pace, but by a shout every now and then, still keep him going and from pulling up altogether, either to get his wind again or for sneaking off among thick high grass and bushes.

Hog will readily take to water to choke off their pursuers, but it is rarely too deep or far to follow. They stick to the banks of big rivers or ravines, on the steep sides of which innumerable small water courses and fissures all running into the main stream at right angles are to be met with every few yards. These perfect chasms, more or less deep and wide, are mostly covered with long dry grass, so many tumbles occur from stumbling into them unawares, and they are often very difficult to get clear from, horse and rider getting wedged in; the boar knows all these little traps by heart and clears them at an easy stride without fail. Falls-out "pig-sticking" are very common occurrences to every one. "Never to let go the bridle" if possible, is the golden rule, while to be pulled off the horse either by its racing under low boughs or diving through the thick "wait-a-bit" thorn bushes is not unusual. Horses that have been raced are the worst for this sport—they simply run away on hearing the other horse by their side, and fancying they are on a smooth flat race course bolt headlong, utterly regardless of the direction the hog may have taken. This sort of blind flight is pretty sure to end in a smash, generally over the edge of some deep ravine not noticed until too late or impossible to pull up at. The rider's seat for this rough work is by no means an upright one, as if taking a park canter and as mostly depicted, but is of the "stick on as you best can" nature, for the whole run is a scramble from beginning to end, and at the finish one has a very misty idea of how half its difficulties were got over.

The horses have now recovered their wind, thorns are picked out, the blood specks from this cause being very conspicuous on grey horses, girths are tightened, and the riders again mounted. The dead boar's legs are tied together two and two with ropes or the bark stripped from some stout young sapling cut down with the beaters' axes, ready to be run through the hog's legs, when men enough have come up to be able to lift him. Perhaps only the boar's head has been cut off to secure the tusks from getting broken. The best plan to secure these is either to leave the skull until it becomes much tainted, when the tusks can be pushed back by a little shaking, being now loose in their sockets, or by well cooking the head, when the same result will be obtained. The tusks must on no account be pulled out as a tooth is, or the thicker ends embedded in the jaw will be broken off. Smashing up the jaw-bones with a chopper is also almost certain to splinter the tusks, and so spoil them for setting as ornaments mounted in silver, as wine labels, sporting trophies, &c.

The beaters have well cleared the first cover or cane field of hog by this time, and the pigs are not likely to visit it again in a hurry, for nothing seems to scare them so much as being hunted with horsemen. Firing at them nightly and perhaps shooting one or more every time seems to have no effect upon the others; for this reason the owners of crops are always glad to send for the sportsmen, besides they are well rewarded for so doing, for in all "hunts" a "fund" is kept up by subscription, to pay for "news" being brought in, and to pay for the beaters required to drive out the hog, also for a good "shikarree" or two, sharp clever native trackers or hunters, whose business it is to make themselves acquainted with the whereabouts or haunt of every big boar for miles round in the neighbourhood. This they do most effectually, many of the old boars being often well known locally by some nickname or other acquired by some extra enormity or long course of evil conduct and cunningness.

The other two sets of riders have also had their respective boars to follow, perhaps as soon as, or very shortly after the two first horsemen have started, for hog seldom break cover simultaneously or at the same point exactly, each seemingly trusting to the better chances of escaping in the confusion by taking a different line of country of his own, and each couple of hunters have in turn their work fully cut out for them, as shown in Plate V., where a charging boar is doing his best to upset horse and rider, as sometimes occurs, and has happened to myself in spite of the spear going right through the hog! With a charging boar the great object is to keep the spear's point low enough, otherwise by knocking it aside with his snout or by pushing it up with the fore part of his long bony head, he will get in under the spear and cut the horse severely, leaving a long ugly wound or piece of flesh scooped out. Horses are usually upset or rolled over by the boar stopping dead short during a run, having pulled up suddenly behind some high bush, and then taking a vicious spring or leap out at the horse in passing, for the strength and weight of a large hog are something tremendous, in his determined charge home.

Talking of upsets, having once, when a frantic "griffin," in company with two others equally green and new to the

Maj. Gen. W. Rice, Delt. Shaw & Sons, Lith.

A CHARGING BOAR

sport, several times slightly speared an old boar, he at length pulled up in a large thorn bush, and refused to again show himself in spite of stones innumerable showered in by the Bheel beaters. At last all three "griffs" (of whom the writer was the middlemost or centre file), agreed to go in at him on foot, shoulder to shoulder, with the spears at the "charge" position, though the men all in vain tried to dissuade us from this most foolish attempt. Having formed up in line just opposite the bush, all ready with spear points well levelled low, we had only advanced a pace or two, when out came the hog with a burst, as if shot from some engine! There was a great cracking of bamboos, and in less than a second all three "griffs" were sprawling on the ground. For my part, the first intimation of what had occurred was seeing the whole landscape suddenly reversed, while performing a complete compulsory somersault; the other two files fell backwards right and left. On scrambling to our feet again the boar was found to have magnanimously backed into the big bush, instead of ripping each of his fallen foes. All the spears were broken, but each had gone well into the pork, as was shown by the blood marks high up.

During a consultation held at a safe distance as to what was next to be done, a great flurry inside the bush proclaimed to our joy that the pig was it its dying struggle; by thus impaling himself he had committed suicide, but the men still looked grave at such folly on our part. One of the riders in the picture has come to grief at a nullah, but that is nothing—he will pick himself and horse up and join in the run again as if nothing had happened, well knowing "good hunters must have falls."

Again to find hog, a line of beaters with the horsemen between them at long intervals, two and two spears in company so as to start fair, will sometimes walk silently across a great stretch of country where pig are known to lie up in bushes during the middle or heat of the day, a mere thrust being given by the beaters with their long bamboo poles at any likely looking spot in passing.

Boars are often roused in this manner quite in the open plain, and splendid runs can then be had, those nearest the boar started giving chase. All will be pretty sure to have their turn in time. Again, in this formation the pig can be tracked at the very early dawn, by the long marks they have left in the grass heavy with the over-night's dew. Great silence must be kept at this work, no neighing steed or talking men, or the swine would get off far out of reach, for they are most quick-hearing animals and cunning beyond belief. Or else a single boar can be "pugged up," that is, have his every footstep followed from some field where he has been feeding during the night, up to the very spot he has chosen to sleep in during the day. Good trackers at this work will not only tell the hog's age and size, but describe him by some nickname, if known to frequent the neighbourhood, never by mistake following up a sow's prints, for they, having no tusks to fight with, and not being always slim enough or fit to run, are never molested, though a lanky old sow can go far longer and give a faster run than a heavy old boar as a rule.

Sometimes on being aroused from his slumbers a big boar will disdain to fly; out he rushes from his lair with a succession of loud startling grunts, the "wough, wough!" aforesaid, and begins charging the first horse he sees, then another, until having run himself high up on everbody's spear, he rolls over dead. No squeak or squeal will ever escape such a truly grand, game, brave fighting animal, though one so much hated and despised in his own country, for his general name, "soor," is no compliment (the tame pig, a horrid brute in every respect, being mostly thereby understood).

Hog are revengeful and particularly savage when hunted,

though at other times they would give people a wide berth. A wounded boar having once given a party of us the slip in some thick jungle, presently terrible yells and screams were heard from a distance behind; on quickly riding up we found an unlucky cultivator at plough had been knocked over, his pair of bullocks with the slight wooden plough at their heels were still scampering round the small enclosed field, while the boar stood over the fallen man and was making vicious rips at his head; luckily this poor fellow had tumbled into a deep ridge or furrow, and was lying flat as possible and bawling at his utmost pitch. The hog was soon driven off and killed, when the patient was found to have only a few skin-deep cuts across and across the head, but bleeding frightfully—a most wonderful escape for his life, owing to his being in the hollow place the boar could not get a proper scoop at his skull.

The most aged boar I ever saw was of a dirty grey colour all over, like an old worn-out white felt hat, having hardly any bristles anywhere, and was the ugliest object possible. Some men cutting sugar cane came in to complain that there was a big brute lying up in one corner of the field, that would allow no one to come near without rushing at them. A large "sounder" had been previously driven off, but this one hog remained in spite of every attempt to dislodge him. Unfortunately all my spears had been sent on to the next halting place, but as a substitute one of the Bheel guards' bayonets was rigged up on a stout pole and well ground to a point on some stones; with this clumsy weapon I started for the field. The patch of uncut cane was not more than five yards square at most. A few blank musket shots accompanied with an extra heavy volley of stones started the pig at last. He was very thin, mere skin and bone, and made off at no pace down a long straight lane with high banks on both sides. On coming up to him, the bayonet instead of going in, merely left a long white streak down his flank; this was repeated four or five times, at each dig the boar jumped up at the horse, and I could both hear and feel the blow given, which sounded like a hard heavy bump rather. The horse set to kicking the boar, who would now run no further, but kept dodging round and round in a circle. My arm was so tired out I could no longer hardly lift the spear, and was each time nearly rolled out of the saddle on trying to use it against such a tough monster, for the point was too blunt to go in at all, and would merely scratch his hide. The pig at length waddled into a muddy pool of water, and as nothing would make him move again, clods and large stones in showers being alike in vain, he was shot there at the earnest entreaty of the cultivators, who did not want to be again troubled with such a demon. Both his tusks were broken off short, luckily for the horse, on whose stomach were long bare marks ending in tufts of hair! This horse would never even look at a hog again, and became most timid, shying at any black object, though a famous steady hunter before. This boar might have been any age, all his bones stuck out, altogether a most ugly brute.

A full-grown hog does not even fear the tiger, for they are sometimes turned out of the same patch of jungle, though sows and squeakers often afford the tiger a chance of food. Once proof was given me that a monster boar was more than a match for a very large lion. While silently following up the prints of a wounded "sambur" (elk), in the Gheer Forest, Kattywar, my men, a little way in the rear, suddenly called to me to "look out." They had disturbed an immense boar asleep in a high "corinda bush" I had just before passed by; there was just time to wheel round sharp and fire both rifle barrels as he came on straight towards me, when he luckily rolled over and down a steep bank dead. On going up we found the hog's back full of deep long furrows, as if some one had dug the iron spikes of a large garden rake well down into his flesh, and then dragged it out sideways; this was at once pronounced by the hunters to be the work of a lion's claws, who had most likely tried to pounce on the boar asleep. Next morning at dawn I shot the lion also, within half a mile of the spot where the wounded hog had been lying up; the lion had a deep cut under the left elbow, around which it had licked off and turned back the hair still wet with its tongue. This wound all agreed was a rip from a boar's tusk, and given no doubt by the one we had found so scored on its back.

A race of grain carriers called "Brinjarees," who are constantly travelling about the country with droves of cattle laden with corn, &c., in sacks, manage to kill hogs with a very large broad barbed spear, the head of which is quite eighteen inches long, and six wide at the barb nearly, with a short staff of about four feet, loaded at the base with a heavy iron ball and spike, the weapon they usually carry. These people have a very fierce set of dogs of a peculiar breed always with them; these dogs soon run any boar found in the jungles by the wayside to bay, and even hold him until their owners come up attracted by the loud barking and grunting going on. The man now hurls this heavy spear most dexterously into the boar's shoulders or flank, while it is still worried by the hounds, taking good care to leap on one side on throwing the spear from only two or three yards distance, but these men sometimes get ripped by the hog at this game.

The pork of a young boar fed on sugar cane, corn, &c., is not bad eating, but it must not be more than two years old or thereabouts. The old pigs had better not be touched, for they have a habit of feeding on any dead animal found, though this cannot often be the case. A friend once told me that while waiting over the newly killed body of a large camel, for a panther that had done the mischief, and was expected to return in the evening, suddenly the camel seemed alive and began to heave up and down; on going close up to see, a large boar rushed out of the camel's inside, on which he had been busily feeding! After that no more wild pork for any one, if you please! It would take a volume to describe all the various incidents, accidents, and experiences that fall to every one's lot on the subject of "pig-sticking," so this must suffice for the present.

CHAPTER V.

CHEETAL SHOOTING.

DESCRIPTION OF AXIS, OR SPOTTED DEER—LARGE HERDS PACKING TOGETHER—PANTHERS' HABITS—GOATS AS LIVE BAIT FOR SAME—HUNTING CHEETA—WILD BUFFALO—WILD DOG—IMPROMPTU LUNCH IN WOODS.

(Plate VI. shows a herd of Cheetal reposing under a wide-spreading shady Bur Tree.)

A FEW days' leave from camp can be passed very pleasantly in "cheetal" shooting. Sending on your small tent, or "rowtee," and all requisite kit a few days beforehand, and then, by placing horses at different stages on the road, follow to the ground, in one long ride, shortly afterwards.

This arrangement will generally be found the best for insuring a fair amount of sport, for it is not likely that these fine deer will be found in any number near any station, on account of the incessant persecution they would suffer from the hands of native hunters or "shikarrees," as well as all who could make sure of a shot within reach of a morning's ride. They are to be found near some camps, but only in single herds, and then dreadfully wild and knowing from constant hunting. For this reason a few friends and self have often ridden over one hundred miles in a day on relays of horses, to overtake the men and baggage sent forward, well into the heart of some lovely distant jungles, rarely disturbed by the presence of man, where each rifle, by a little labour, could ensure twelve shots of a morning, at as many different herds, or solitary scattered bucks therefrom, for the deer literally swarmed.

There not being sufficient inhabitants in these wild districts, it well answered to take three or four willing young men, well up in sporting matters, with each gun, so as to be independent. A cart-load of grain, tobacco, food, &c., would also be sent on for the use of these native hunters, enough, with the bountiful supply of meat obtained, to keep all hands very contented and glad to join in such an "outing." By changing ground a few miles every other day or so, fresh, undisturbed "happy hunting grounds" could be shot over. The baggage, skins, horns, &c., following on the few camels required, for, of course, every one travels in the lightest possible marching order on these occasions.

In some parts of these forests herds of thirty or forty "cheetal" deer would be seen, grouped under the large spreading boughs of some fine gigantic trees, standing apart, in what looked really park-like scenery, for open undulating glades would be frequently met with in places otherwise surrounded by the densest jungle. Here, under every smaller shady tree, standing by itself on the grass-covered plain, would also be two or three bucks separated from the larger herds—a beautiful sight, but rather puzzling to decide which group it would be best to attempt getting within range of; a point to be settled by the direction of the wind, if any, and cover afforded for stalking purposes. The deer like these open places, for, by being able to see clear all round, they are safe from the attacks of their numerous enemies always on the watch for a chance of stealing upon them unawares, such as tigers, panthers, wolves, wild dogs, and, lastly, the sportsman himself.

First, to describe the "cheetal" or "spotted deer" (of which species of axis it is supposed there are two kinds). The largest, or that found in Central India, and the splendid preserves for all sorts of stags on the banks of the grand "Taptee" and "Nurbudda" rivers, would stand about three

Maj. Gen. W. Rice, Delt. Shaw & Sons, Lith.

A HERD OF "CHEETAL" OR "SPOTTED DEER"

feet three inches high, and be about five feet in length. They remind one at first sight very much of the "fallow deer" in English parks, but instead of wide, palmated horns, have straight, rather smooth horns, about two feet three inches long, or more, with only two tines, one about a foot from the top, and the lower one about two inches from the burr or base; these horns are curved most gracefully, and spread about twenty inches apart at the points; they are shed afresh every year, the bucks alone, of course, bearing them. The bucks and does are alike, of a red fawn colour, with lines of white spots on their flanks, lengthways, and a dark, almost black band along their backs and neck, black muzzle, but white in front of neck or throat, along the stomach, and inside the thighs, with a rather long tail, red above, but with long white hairs below; this they spread out, and flap up and down on moving off very conspicuously.

These deer are fond of water, so are never found very far away from the banks of rivers well shaded with jungle trees. It is a pretty sight to see them come down to drink—after all collecting in a body on the high banks of the stream, first a single big buck runs down to the water from out of the thick jungle or cover that has partially concealed them; after staring about him on both sides for a minute or so, he lowers his head to drink, when instantly all the rest of the herd come bounding down the banks, and closing round the buck in a compact mass, also begin drinking without any hesitation, or first looking round; presently they all wheel round, and, springing up the banks again, are soon lost to sight in the woods.

The best time to start for shooting these bucks is the moment it is light enough to see them; they will then be found in the more open parts of the woods grazing, in parties of five or six, or else a single buck will be met with, at intervals of every quarter of a mile or so. As the sun gets up, and the day becomes hot, they hide away in the thick covers for shelter in the numerous ravines, all leading down towards the big river on both banks, and when started therefrom, rush off in a wild manner, that affords only a snap shot, with little chance of picking out the finest pair of horns, whereas, when they can be found busy grazing and alone, a steady telling shot can be taken at any particularly fine head of antlers. There is no need to fire at every one met with, better wait till you can come up with a real beauty; and it is astonishing how soon one becomes quite indiffent to any but the most perfect specimens when there is such ample choice to select from.

I once shot a very old buck, with extraordinary long single horns, without any signs of the upper tines, most curious to look at. If merely so disturbed, and not shot at, these deer do not go far, but start off at a bounding pace, and then suddenly stop, and wheel round for a prolonged stare, looking over the tops of some low bushes, or standing in patches of high grass, perfectly immovable, at about a hundred yards distance, making it very difficult to again distinguish them, for the head and horns are thrown well back, and all to be seen is the black muzzle, large eyes, white ears, and a little of the white throat; the rest is high dry grass or leaves, not much of a mark to aim at, but sufficient. There is a tremendous "flop" noise, but the buck itself has disappeared, as if by magic. On walking up, reloaded, of course, it is found lying flat and stunned in the long grass, seemingly dead; but don't trust to appearances, but, taking care to keep well clear of his horns and hoofs, out with the big sharp hunting knife, and cut his throat at once—high up, just under the the lower jaw. The skin round the upper part of the neck is very thick and tough, so the ball often glances, when there is a deal of blood to be seen about everywhere, but no deer; and the worst of it is, he will so run for miles, and often then get clear off.

If a shot can be had at a buck quietly grazing, take him well forward behind the shoulder, half way up the depth of the body, when it will roll over, with a vast amount of kicking and plunging; but a wound in the stomach or hind quarters as the deer move off, is of little use, for they are almost sure to get clear away, of course only to die afterwards; but then the horns are lost—always a cause of grief, for one can't help fancying them finer than they perhaps really were—for the lost fish is always the biggest!

When deer are come upon while grazing, especially if alone, or only a few bucks in company, and seen from a distance, there is plenty of time to take a good view of them through the small pocket telescope, so as to mark the best horns, for they seldom raise their heads above half a foot from the ground, but go mooning on at a very slow foot's-pace, cropping a fresh green blade here and there on either side; of course the greatest care must be taken to be perfectly silent, and that no sudden jerky movement is made by self or men, or the telescope flashed about; and above all that you are working towards the deer against the wind; to gain which most important point, a wide circle had better be made on first viewing the stags, so as to be able to get within shooting distance without giving them that fatal chance of being aware of your presence. Often only part of a buck may be viewed from a distance while grazing on the new sprouting blades of grass, freshly sprung up in open spaces where the jungle grass has been fired, the rest of his body hidden by some intervening wide tree trunk or stump. Now a famous chance presents itself for getting close up, by keeping this particular tree, or any others on the way, between yourself and the unconscious deer, as you pick your way on tip-toe, or crouching low down as possible to within a certain and most easy killing distance. Slowly peering round the tree trunk, bare headed, and with only half an eye, is an anxious moment, often only to view the stag racing off in safety, an unlucky stumble, or some such noise, having scared him, or, quite as likely, the alarm has been given by some horrid bird flying past, chattering or screaming most loudly, as if in the utmost terror.

Deer and game generally seem to the outwitted sportsman to have very many such allies as these. The prettily spotted skins of these "axis" deer make nice rugs for floors, or mats rather. A picked shot can sometimes be got at these deer as they troop off at a trot on being disturbed, for they will often stop for a short look round on hearing the loud whistle before mentioned, or the "cluck, cluck" noise loudly given, such as natives use to urge on their bullocks, for they are accustomed to this sound in places where gangs of wood cutters are employed in clearing the forest timber, as it is constantly used to encourage the cattle when hauling logs or any such work. I have seen a herd of "cheetal" quite three hundred strong, if not more, moving slowly along an open part of the forest at different times. About a dozen large bucks were leading close together, their mass of horns making a grand show; then came does and fawns, of all sizes, mixed up together, in the middle, while about fifteen or more other fine stags brought up the rear of this column, quite a hundred yards in length, by about thirty yards in width. This marching mass is not usual, but had no doubt been caused by the deer being so constantly fired at for several days in succession, when all the small parties got together for protection.

When, after looking everywhere all the morning for deer, and none are to be seen, it may be concluded that they have taken to "packing" in this fashion, and that it is time to try new ground much farther off. When, peering about, at a foot's pace, in the early dawn, with only one sharp-eyed "shikarree" by one, eagerly looking over the edge of each ravine as the banks are reached, often the buck will be the first to spy you, when a loud kind of barking note will be uttered by him, as a signal of danger being near, and a warning to all other deer within hearing—for they make just the same loud sharp sound when a tiger is seen moving about the jungle, as well as on catching sight of a man. All sportsmen should be able to imitate this call; it is easily learnt, and constantly used by hunters when in the woods, on their getting separated from each other, or wishing to call attention without the chance of scaring away any game that might be near, by the human voice. Your companion answers it from the distance, just as the deer do on hearing one another call or bellow, when on you go again, or wait for any one to join company. It is often necessary to work a little apart in the woods, especially when taking up prints or the blood of a wounded animal; but being once apart it is not so easy to always again meet, when the feeling of being lost or not knowing well in which direction to keep moving on is decidedly unpleasant. Every one takes care to instantly answer this note by a similar call, for instead of your companion it may truly be the warning of a buck having seen something dangerous, and best to be prepared for, with a rifle at the "ready." The big "samber" (elk) deer also makes this row, even louder, called "poopah" by the natives, and the little "beekree," or "jungle sheep," does it on all occasions, at night even, and is so called the "barking deer."

The other sort of "cheetal" referred to is found in Southern India, and is smaller in size every way, with shorter horns, of a rougher appearance. The meat of these deer is very coarse, and requires plenty of sauce to make it palatable. The panther often succeeds in pouncing on a doe cheetal, that, with the rest of the herd, has come down to drink. It is observed by old hunters that a doe is almost invariably the victim in these cases, the panther doubtless having a proper dread of the sharp horns of the buck, while, perhaps, the doe may be more tender to eat.

PANTHER SHOOTING.

Panthers have a habit of lurking in this manner ready to drop down on any game passing below. They climb the high waving clumps of bamboos, lying hid among the leaves and overhanging long branches, matted together, monkeys especially being considered fair game. The newly-arrived sportsman had better be very careful on meeting with one of these most dangerous brutes, for they are very difficult to kill dead, and are almost certain to charge home on being wounded, with lightning rapidity, giving no time to change empty cartridges, or get hold of a spare gun. They seem for the time bullet proof, unless of course a shot at the head can be secured; but that is a very small mark in a hurry. A shot well forward in the shoulders will roll them over, but must be repeated as quickly as possible, for this beast's strength and activity are something wonderful; an astonishing number of badly wounded ones getting away, of course to die afterwards, in caves generally, compared with those that are shot dead. It is very rare to find old gun-shot wounds or other hurts on these animals.

There is some doubt as to whether there is more than one sort of panther, the smaller variety called the "leopard" being considered the same, but with certain distinctive points owing to age, locality, &c. There certainly is a very marked difference in their appearance, the one being short, stout, of a bright yellow, with close-lying short hair, much resembling in build a small tigress—indeed one of the native names for this beast is the "half tiger;" while the other is a long, thin, lithe looking animal of a grey colour, with a far longer tail, and the hair seems rather curly or even woolly. There is a marked difference in the spots also. The first named brute is decidedly the most awkward to encounter, and its fierceness is such that I was once assured of one that was known while courting a tigress (by mistake it was supposed), to have kept for several days all male tiger suitors at a distance. This fact was believed to be the case by the loud constant quarrelling of the rivals, and the panther being seen to keep the lady all to himself! After this a new animal for the Zoological Gardens ought to turn up some fine day. By always attentively listening to any information these men of the woods may have to impart, either of their personal experience or from tradition, a truly wonderful stock of most curious hunting lore is to be obtained, the chief difficulty being often what to really believe or discredit entirely. No attempt at ridicule or doubt must ever be expressed, or the narrators will at once become silent and refrain from ever afterwards mentioning any curious fact well worth hearing.

A full-grown panther will be quite eight feet long, and stand about two feet three inches high, but it is so rare to see them except in a low crouching creeping attitude. One seen walking unconcernedly along a wide path once was mistaken by me for a tigress, until it came so close that the spots could be distinguished. In the bright glare of the sun and towards the end of the hot season, when all animals have their thinnest coats on, and the markings become more faded, often from age, it is not always possible to be certain at any little distance what game has been started; shape and peculiar gait are then the only tests to judge by.

Panthers are quite capable of killing cattle, ponies, half-grown pigs, and all kinds of deer, and are occasionally known to kill people asleep. This sort of murderer is very much dreaded, for these beasts wander about villages at night as much at home and fearless as if in the woods. I have seen small places of a few huts only, entirely deserted and left to ruin, solely from the repeated visits of a single panther. In sheds where goats are secured at night, they will think nothing of tearing a hole down through the roof, and on getting inside are pretty sure to kill the whole flock, out of mere wantonness. A goat owner once described to me a scene of this kind: he hid himself in a large earthern jar used for storing grain in, being unarmed and powerless to prevent the slaughter going on, and prayed for dawn, when the panther took himself off. Dogs are a very common prey of these brutes; they make any peculiar noise at dark just outside the village, when out run the usual pack of curs all barking at once, when a victim is easily secured. A friend mentioned having seen three young panthers jump down from a large shady tree, upon the low branches of which they had been eating a village dog, taken up there for the purpose, while on two occasions I have known English dogs to be carried off by panthers from the very midst of our party of sportsmen, where their servants, huntsmen, horses, camels, &c., were encamped around, and the like fate has befallen tame goats belonging to the same camp, though firmly picketed or tied down to pegs at night.

In the "Dandilli jungles," near Camp Belgaum, a rock is shown, where a panther on going down to drink at the river, was seized by the forepaw by an alligator, and after a long struggle pulled under the deep water and no doubt eaten at leisure. The panther's cries called out the whole village to witness this tragedy, but no assistance was given him!

Plate VIII. shows how camels even are killed by panthers, which happened several times to my knowledge in "Western Kattywar," and used to be a subject of much wonderment

Maj. Gen. W. Rice, Del.

Shaw & Sons, Lith.

CAMEL ATTACKED BY PANTHER

until the owners had described witnessing the whole performance. My first impression was that the camels had been jumped upon, as the lion in Africa is said to serve the giraffe, and after a long ride had been borne down, but the men declared the panther showed himself before the grazing camel, and after rolling itself in a ball and playing many such odd tricks before the camel, would by degrees roll over close to its feet, when on the camel stretching down its neck to smell, or out of curiosity examine this strange object, it was at once seized by the throat, and after much violent tossing about of the enemy, was in the end fairly pulled down on its knees and killed. I have watched over dead camels thus fresh killed, and seen the panther return at dusk for his meal; he comes out of the jungle running on calling out in a pleased manner, with tail perfectly erect, just as a tame cat does for a saucer of milk; on hearing this sound, the jackals that have been previously busy tearing at the dead animal, at once retire to a respectful distance, sitting round in a half circle.

This plan of watching for panthers is very commonly carried out every evening by sportsmen, when in the jungles or places where panthers are known to frequent. A goat is generally tied up very firmly to a short peg, when the gunner ensconces himself behind some natural screen, such as a thick bush, taking care not to much alter its usual appearance, though for better concealment he may add a few fresh boughs to peep through. This can be all arranged close to where the tents with their numerous noisy followers have been pitched during the day. The panther has been waiting till dusk fully intending to visit this encampment in the evening, and is almost certain to come down from any hills close by or out of the surrounding jungle just as twilight sets in. You have not long to wait—the goat or sheep somehow seems to be aware of the enemy's presence, and becomes silent but restless; before this the louder the goat has been calling, as they will do on being separated from their fellows, the better, for it at once attracts the panther. Some goats after being used for this little game several times, become so knowing, it is said, as to remain silent altogether, as if with the wilful intention of spoiling sport, when a fresh goat must be substituted. The panther will now come creeping noiselessly as possible out of the bushes close by, for the goat should not be tied up in too open a spot, and sit down opposite to reconnoitre its victim, when bang! goes a shell into its chest, followed by another quickly as the smoke will allow, fired from only a dozen yards or so off by the concealed marksman. It is as well to have more than one gun handy for the work, and be quick in giving the other spare barrels, for often with a sudden bound the panther picks himself up and dashes back into the jungle, when there is nothing for it but to wait till daylight next morning for a search.

After once losing a fine panther fired at in this manner the previous evening, I turned out with merely slippers and scanty undress on at dawn next morning, to find if possible any blood or other marks, taking merely my short double rifle. There was a mound close by formed by an old white ants' nest, out of which grew a fine wide "corindah bush," with thick overhanging foliage; on nearing this some monkeys in a mango tree overhead commenced swearing or uttering their peculiar harsh cry of alarm and warning most loudly, but concluding that they were merely calling at me, I had crawled on hands and knees under the bush, as a likely spot to examine for blood or prints of the overnight's panther, that had bounded off in this direction. Presently on looking up carelessly, there were the panther's fore paws to be seen within six inches of my face; a further silent glance showed the brute lying full length on the smoothed top of the mound, its eyes half closed and looking very seedy indeed, for there was a neat round hole, from which blood trickled, in the very centre of its chest. Silently putting the butt of the short rifle on the ground, and bringing the muzzle round to bear on the panther's throat, almost touching it, I cocked one barrel, and tapping the trigger, blew him off backwards with a shell. A friend who had also turned out in deshabille to help look for prints on the wet dewy grass, concluded the gun had gone off by accident, for I fell flat instantly on firing to avoid a possible mauling by the panther. This was a very lucky escape, for had the brute known I was there, a blow from his awful paws and bite or two from equally terrible jaws, would surely have followed. The monkeys evidently knew of the panther's presence, and were swearing at him not myself. All this took place within about sixty paces of the tents.

Panthers are often to be found in sugar cane fields, but it is almost impossible to get them out of such dense cover, so high overhead too generally. A good deal of noise, stone throwing in volleys, and blank shots from matchlocks, with some native-made rockets thrown in, may give a chance of a snap bounding shot as the beast makes off for any adjoining cover close by, in which direction the attempt to drive him should always be made, for it is hopeless to expect the animal to break towards the open plain, as is mostly foolishly tried. It is simple madness to try and walk in after the lurking brute, for once in sugar cane all is dark, and the gunner might tread on the crouching panther before it would move; nor can a gun be used in such extra close cover, nor is it fair to urge or expect the beaters to enter such a stronghold as these cane fields form. This is the commonest kind of accident, very seldom attempted too without ending in failure, for if the beast is started by a rocket, &c., it instantly plunges back into another equally thick corner of the cover. This case is as hopeless as trying to shoot a panther while in its cave; it is simply invisible in almost every instance.

Native chiefs, on a panther being tracked to his den, sometimes have him blocked in with piles of cut bushes, grass, &c. A few days afterwards these are set on fire, when possibly a shot may be had at the half-starved thirsty animal as it bolts out, but this is hardly sport. The art of skinning and pegging out the panther's beautiful skin will be mentioned hereafter.

There is another variety of panther called the "black leopard," but very rarely met with. It has a skin of dull black colour throughout, the spots showing only in a particular light, and then only faintly. "The cheetah" is the name by which all panthers and leopards are commonly known in India, but such local names as "tendooah," "bimptee," by the Bheels, and "deeprah" of Guzeerat are also applied to this animal, which however must in no way be confounded with the "cheeta," or "hunting leopard," a very inferior spotted animal that no one ever cares to shoot. They are sometimes to be met with in open bushy plains, where in parties of five or less they hunt the gazelle, "chinkarra," also black buck, "nil-ghai," and at times turn their attention to sheep also, just as "wolves" do, and their method of hunting is precisely similar.

Having found the deer or intended game, they spread out in a good wide circle, when one of the gang will make a rush at the deer, and as it races off the rest of the "cheetas" also take up the running, jumping out of any bush at the scared quarry as it passes their respective hiding-places. Of course, this unfair style of coursing sooner or later succeeds. On one occasion, thus meeting with a batch of five hunting leopards in a good open plain, our party tried to ride them down and spear them—for we were looking for hog at the time; but they were far too quick for our good horses, cantering along just out of spear-reach quite easily, and even looking round or back. On coming to a large, deep, well-wooded ravine they slunk off down it quite leisurely.

This "cheeta" is a long, slim, graceful animal, standing about two feet two inches high, with a tail almost as long as its body. It has a very tucked-up appearance, like a greyhound, and is covered with single spots. Its claws are not retractile, but like a dog's. The general colour is red fawn, with two very marked black streaks down the face from the eyes, little round ears, with a short hog mane and rather long woolly hair under the stomach. Young ones are now and then found by grass-cutters, and can be easily tamed as pets. These are the animals used by native chiefs to hunt the numerous almost tame black buck they keep in large preserves for the purpose. The sport is carried on from a cart, and is well known.

In the country between the two rivers "Taptee" and "Nurbudda," previously mentioned, will be found the "wild buffalo," far beyond "Asseerghur Fort;" but I never had the good fortune to meet with one, although shooting several times over these splendid jungles. This animal more porperly belongs to the Bengal Presidency, so no description will be here attempted of how to hunt it. I have seen the immensely stout bones of this huge brute lying in the woods; they formed the subject of very serious conversation always among my men, who seemed to dread this big bull greatly, standing over six feet high, and used to describe its savage looks, with bushy locks between the eyes and tufts of hair on the knees. These bones were supposed to be the remains of victims killed by a joint attack of two or three tigers, for the bull was always spoken of as being more than a match for any single tiger.

In these same jungles I several times met with "wild dogs," sometimes in packs of twenty, or again a single one, and once almost stepped on a mother with four little puppies, that ran yelping and squeaking in and out of a patch of high dry grass they were lying up in. My man was up a tree like lightning on this occasion, saying he fully expected we should be attacked by several other dogs, but none appeared. Again, hearing a loud yelping noise coming on through the woods, we stood still close by a large tree, and then saw a pack of quite thirty or more of these jungle dogs in full cry after a fine buck samber, that was only about fifty yards ahead of them. They passed us without taking the slightest notice, and we could hear their cry in the far distance. The pace was very good indeed; a wide, deep nullah or ravine was taken in full stride—altogether a very pretty sight. These wild dogs differed in appearance from some I have seen in more Southern India, particularly in having their full brushy tail tipped most plainly with black, and seemed less lanky and of a darker reddish-brown. I have shot both for examination only. It is merely mentioned here as one of the wild animals a stranger may expect to fall in with in Indian forests. These dogs are well known to hunt tigers, and cause them to seek safety by climbing trees—a most unusual circumstance for the tiger, and one that clearly proves his dread of such formidable foes.

I was once gravely informed of a case of a pack of wild dogs having so treed a tiger; while all were jumping up and baying at him, one of their number happened to stake himself behind on the stalk of some thick "carwar" brushwood (a stout, tall, Jerusalem artichoke sort of plant, with which the hills and jungles in parts are covered for miles upon miles), and which the pack of hounds had trampled down in their attempts to reach the tiger. This accident caused the wild dog such agony, that his cries drove away the rest of his companions; but the tiger, still seeing this impaled dog, though now quite dead, stuck upright below the tree, was afraid to descend, lest the supposed sentinel should at once recall his friends. The end was, that the tiger also died up the tree from thirst, hunger, and fright combined! and his body was found jammed between two wide branching forks of the tree, much swollen and with swarms of flies around it. Two wood-cutters, who had bolted on first hearing the baying of the pack of wild dogs, discovered this tragedy on passing the spot some few days afterwards!

Walking through these lovely forests from earliest dawn in constant expectation of meeting something worth shooting, causes the time to slip by quite unheeded. Before now, on looking at my watch, I have been surprised to find it two o'clock before breakfast, and in consequence become terribly hungry all of a sudden. Should nothing else be forthcoming—for one often sets out intending to take merely a short stroll before returning to the small tent, but is led away by some long unexpected chase presenting itself—the liver of the "cheetal" or "samber" can always be cut out, a fire of dry grass and leaves at once made, and squares of the liver, about two inches each, covered over in the ashes of the impromptu fire, will soon cook beautifully, the smell telling when they are done to a turn. They are now raked out with a stick, all the outer parts cut off with a knife, and there is breakfast ready. A little mixture from one's flask and the clear water from the nearest river completes the meal, when the tired sportsman, who otherwise would very likely knock up if longer famished, having possibly many miles to find his way back, can continue his hunting as fresh as on setting out. In the supposed absence of lucifer matches, a pinch of gunpowder, with or without a gun-cap, rolled up in a shred of rag and struck on a stone by another heavy stone with a drawing blow will light at once; or a like shred of turban cloth can be squibbed from the gun with the merest pinch of powder, and caught ablaze when falling earthwards; or the end of one's telescope will act as a burning glass in about a minute or two. Of course, these mild little dodges are merely mentioned for the veriest novice, who, however, will often find the men with him pestering for fire to light their "beerees" or leaf-made pipes. This smoking practice had better be deferred till the hunt or stalk is over, for the deer well know what the smell of tobacco means, and vanish forthwith.

CHAPTER VI.

BEAR HUNTING.

THE INDIAN BLACK BEAR DESCRIBED — HUNTING PLANS — FATAL SHOTS — SMOKING OUT OF CAVES—BEARS CLIMBING TREES AND ROBBING BEES' NESTS — THE SAMBER (ELK) — DESCRIPTION AND HABITS — STALKING STAGS—AN "UPSET"—SAMBER LEATHER—THE "HOG DEER"—THE FOUR-HORNED ANTELOPE—AN "IBEX?"—THE WILD SHEEP OR RAVINE DEER—THE MOUSE DEER.

(*Plate VII. shows a scene to be sometimes met with in the jungles very early in the morning:—A family party of the "Indian Black Bear" busily feeding on ripe wild figs.*)

RIPE wild fig trees are to be found very commonly scattered over most wild countries, in the thickest forests as well as in more open places. These figs, oddly enough, grow in thick clusters out of the very bark of the large branches, instead of hanging singly from the end of thin boughs. When ripe each tree can be scented a long way off, which no doubt helps to attract the bears. This is also the case with the "mowrah" tree, so very frequently to be seen in some jungles, either standing alone or in small groups. These trees when in full blossom have a very strong perfume, almost sickly, and the small, round, pulpy flower, that when dead-ripe drops to the ground, can be winded a long way. Here these berries, of a pale yellow or nearly white colour, lie in heaps decaying, and so tainting the air that no other scent is noticed during their season of ripening. The natives collect these berries in small baskets, and distil a very strong liquor from them. Nothing seems to attract bears and hog also more than these trees. Samber and cheetal also are often to be seen picking up the fruit, but not in the wholesale manner bears feed upon it. Though out all night long, and from the previous evening on its getting a little cool, roaming everywhere in search of their different kinds of food, such as roots, berries of all sorts, grubs to be found under large stones, that require to be rolled over for the purpose, the larvæ of white ants' nests, &c., bears can only be stumbled upon by the hunter in the earliest part of the day, for directly it begins to get at all warm they hasten to lie up in cool, rocky dens, or under very thick, closely-matted bushes, no doubt their heavy black coats making the heat unbearable. Besides, the ground, especially if at all rocky, becomes far too hot to walk on pleasantly. Some rest time, too, must be needed. In the rainy season they are to be seen out at any hour of the day, but then the woods are not in fit order for hunting.

First, to describe these animals, that afford very good sport, and are the best possible brutes to enter any young hand at or beginner in the noble art of "shikar," or big-game hunting. A full-grown "Indian black bear" will be about six feet long, and stand nearly three feet high. He is one mass of long coarse black hair, rough to a degree, with a thicker, and slightly longer tuft, sticking up on and between the shoulders: his nose, up to between the eyes, is of a dirty white, and there is a letter V or horse-shoe shaped band of the same dirty white on the chest, and white on the end of the toes. His claws are very large and powerful, bent down in a half-circle, five on the fore feet, and five or four only on the hind. There is no mistaking his great, broad foot-print, something like a gigantic human foot, without the toe-marks, but with dents instead, formed by the ends of the much curved claws. These fore-feet prints are much larger than the hind ones, and are turned inwards, while the hind

Maj. Gen. W. Rice, Delt.

Shaw & Sons, Lith.

"INDIAN BLACK BEARS" AND "SAMBER" DEER

feet-marks are always pointing outwards. The arms and fore part of the bear's body give the idea of immense power, while he seems to fall off in the hind quarters. The back is very broad indeed, but with no great depth of body, which is arched considerably; his canine teeth are formidable weapons.

Bears, though not to be named with tigers, panthers, &c., in point of danger, when shot at, can still give a good deal of trouble to kill. This was especially the case before the present immense improvement in all kinds of firearms; compared with the now enormous charges of powder, and bullets or shells, quite four-fold in weight to those formerly in use, when an "18 bore" spherical bullet, with "$1\frac{1}{4}$ dram" of gunpowder, was the load for a double muzzle-loading rifle, about the size of firearms usually carried by all sportsmen, and used by the writer for very many years. In firing at a bear great care should be taken to make the shot as central a one as possible, otherwise there is the chance of the ball whizzing through the great depth of hair only, that makes up quite half the animal's apparent size, especially when its lumbering, most clumsy, shuffling, uneven gait is considered, the course never being straight in any direction, but swaying about, zigzag fashion, every other step, and the pace astonishingly quick for such an ungainly looking brute. For a side shot, just under the forearm, well in the middle of the body, is the best; this will be at once signalled by the loud moaning kind of sigh, rapidly continued, that bears utter on getting a mortal wound, and is pleasant to hear, for it announces that the "kill" is all right, mostly without much trouble following. A side-head shot, about the ears, also well centered, is of course to be preferred, but can seldom be made sure of at this quick dodging beast, constantly swaying its whole body in almost any direction. There is no harm in giving a bear plenty of lead, for though knocked over, and seemingly quite done for, they often pick themselves up and roll off down any steep hill-side, either giving endless trouble to again come up with, or getting clear away.

Again, with this beast too much caution cannot be used to be sure he is really dead, for very many serious accidents have taken place from this mistake, the bear suddenly jumping up as alive as ever, when woe betide any one in his clutches. A good-sized stone or clod of earth, thrown with a will at the prostrate carcase, will be sure to settle any doubts, for the dull bump sound that follows as the stone rebounds, and rolls aside, will be enough to revive or wake up any merely stunned or possibly shamming animal.

Bears are often come upon very close indeed by the hunter, walking, as he always ought, most silently; they are then either asleep in thick bushes during the heat of the day, or so busily engaged in feeding, scratching up the nests of white ants, &c., that they do not keep their usual watchfulness. They have capital scenting powers, and are off at the slightest warning of danger, seeming to trust as much to their ears as eyes, for they may be observed to stop short while bolting away up hill, and listen for a few seconds only, and then on again. A bear's pace up hill is something wonderful, more like an easy canter than climbing, and utterly hopeless to think of competing with so as to head him back, while his rate of getting down hill is to be only equalled by a large stone, for he very often rolls himself up into a perfect ball seemingly, and comes down the steepest places in a series of bumps, alighting on his back or shoulders, unrolling himself, and scrambling off as if nothing had happened, when the life, or breath at least, would have been knocked out of any other animal. When disturbed in this sudden manner, they rush about on all sides, with short, quick runs, first at one person and then another, growling all the time most loudly. This is as much confusion as fear and rage combined, but it often makes shooting them a difficult matter, for, with people scattered all around you, it is unsafe to fire. They generally break back on being so awakened, which makes it awkward enough for any one following, such as spare gun carriers, the water bottle bearer, guides, &c. One is often then obliged to fire in self defence, when it would have been more agreeable to look up the bear at another time, more noble game being, perhaps, in view. They are very obstinate brutes, and not to be turned from their course easily. On more than one occasion I have seen them, in their headlong flight, race over a prostrate man, who had fallen or thrown himself down for safety, unconsciously inflicting severe scratches on these victims.

Bears seem to have an especial dread of fire; lighting the dry grass will invariably send them out, best pace, at the first crackle and smoke of any thick patch they may have pulled up in. These are generally wounded ones, too much hurt to go further; otherwise it is difficult to come up with a wounded bear, for distance seems no object to him when getting out of the rifleman's reach. Firing the jungle should only be resorted to in the most extreme cases, for it is most difficult to afterwards suppress the fire, besides having the evil effect of scaring away all the game for miles round. To drive bears out of caves in which they are known to lie up, or seen to enter, the native-made fireworks are very good, those called "anars," or pomegranates, being best, for they fiz away famously, make an intolerable smoke and smell of brimstone, quite suffocating, besides ending with a very loud bang, blowing splinters of the earthern case they are held in to all corners of a den. This ought to start any bear, or else the native-made rockets, called "bans," can be used; these are better for thickets than caves, for they rush about whizzing in all directions at right angles, ending with a grand explosion. These fireworks require to be handled very cautiously, for sometimes merely lighting the touch-paper fuse is followed by an instant explosion, from the extreme dryness of the material, or bad workmanship. Don't let any one attempt to blow these fireworks into a better light; for I once saw a poor fellow knocked over, frightfully singed, and nearly blinded, from this cause. If one is not sufficient, of course more grenades can be thrown in, but better try in another corner of the cave, if possible.

Most of these natural caves have exits somewhere else, being generally formed of fallen masses of rock, piled in a strange jumble over each other down the mountain's side. Smoke will be seen coming out of these distant places; if not wide enough for the bear to escape by, they point out where to drop in another firework, being most probably the end of some long underground cave. The best plan is to take up a silent position above where the bear is expected to appear; this gives a better view all round, and closer shot, for bears almost invariably bolt up hill on being disturbed, so must pass close to the gunner on guard. I once saw six big and little bears come out of a cave into which only one had been marked down, so it is as well to be prepared for more company arriving than expected.

On hilly, mountainous ground, the usual plan to find bears is to start a set of men off at the very faintest sign of day-break, to take up their positions, two and two, for they always fear to go alone, on all the best and highest peaks around, or the hill-tops, so as to be able to observe any and every moving animal, either below in the plains, or on the hill-sides. By the time the sun gets well up, about 8 a.m. at the latest, all these brutes will have sought shelter of some sort for the day. Some bears will have been seen to enter caves, or pull up in thick clumps of bamboo and other dense, shady bushes. The big samber (elk) will be lying down under some fine shady trees in the open, or else under cover of thick trees on the hill sides, or large detached rocks. Nothing is more interesting than thus watching these animals, quite unconscious of any coming danger to themselves. The best plan, and one that ensures sport, is to accompany the men in a body, for then they can be kept silent, otherwise they will talk, partly from carelessness, and chiefly in self-defence, for, being unarmed, they dread meeting suddenly some tiger, or other brute out for his night's foraging expedition: these men are then dropped at proper intervals of half a mile or more on fitting points, with a clear view around. Remember to start early enough, for it is broad day above on the hills, though dark enough in the valley below, where the tent will most likely be pitched for shade and water sake.

Having gone over the ground on the prevous day perhaps while hunting, will be quite enough to show the sportsman where to select these look-out places, and the men know the way well when they see your intention and object in placing them. It does not take very long, and must be performed in the most perfect silence. Nothing is more satisfactory to all parties, for when all moving animals are marked down, these people have methods, without calling out, which must never be allowed, of signalling to each other; either to keep watch on any particular animal that has moved beyond their point of watching, or that persists in wandering about for an unusually late hour, so that it shall not be able to so escape being also marked down.

Now go round and collect the several reports, silently, of course. Much grinning and silent laughter will be made over this business, as they point to some unsuspicious beast having gone to roost perhaps just below or close to their post. The men can then be silently collected and taken away with you, for they will want to smoke, drink water, feed, or rest.

There is plenty of time for all this, for the hotter the day becomes, the greater the certainty of finding each sleeping beauty. After a consultation, the best and most noble game will be selected,—tiger first, of course, then panther, then bear, and after that, samber, for horns and leather sake, as well as meat for the men. This is the object of going yourself, to see what may be wandering about in the neighbourhood, otherwise only the eatable deer will be mentioned as having been seen. This neglect arises from the people not having the same interest as yourself in the killing of big game, as well, perhaps, as some doubts as to the perfect safety of stirring up any ferocious brute, with, perhaps, but slight knowledge of, or confidence in, the hunter's skill as a marksman. For this purpose it is not a bad plan, unless you happen to be well known to some of the men, as will surely be the case, to let them see that you can hit a small object with certainty. There will be plenty of opportunities of showing this without disturbing the country by unnecessary noise of firing, such as after a day's work, when the guns want cleaning, select some small spot on a tree, or put up a bottle at a safe distance. The effect of the bullets is always a source of wonder to the natives, and being so vastly superior to their own firearms or matchlocks, cannot fail to give them great confidence. Indeed I have known this often to be too great, for they would be apt to consider every animal mortally wounded on discovering the first drop of blood, whereas it may have been only slightly touched, or hit in a wrong part. Two or more shots are enough, but of course extra pains must be taken to ensure "bull's eyes." If any of your own men who have seen you pretty successful at killing game are present, they are sure to inform the strangers, for on this subject a great deal more questioning goes on than is mostly suspected. A bad, or we will say, unlucky shot or marksman, would very likely find that he could not collect the men at all, endless excuses being forthcoming, all but the real one, which politeness would forbid being named.

In the same manner these people are uncommonly sharp at discovering whether the sportsman really knows anything about his business, and will help in proportion. The beginner must not be disheartened at this, for nothing is so easily learnt as the art of hunting, if there is any taste for the amusement. All hands new to the country are sure to make their first few trips under the guidance of some experienced old hunters, who have themselves acquired their knowledge from others long ago. Every day adds to this store of information, and a little practice is then all that is required to turn out the self-confident, keen, indefatigable "shikarree." These wood men will not expect you to be able to "pug," or follow the tracks of any animal, this being the very end and crown of the perfect hunter; but by close observation, on all possible opportunities, it is as well to become acquainted with, or able to form some idea of each beast's footprint, for if they think it can be safely done, the very young hand will be almost certain to have some such deceit played him, as goats' footsteps palmed upon him for the noble boar, which has somehow vanished most unaccountably, while there are stories of a dried tiger's foot being mounted on a stick, which was forthcoming on occasion to show where the monster's fresh prints had been lost by the hard working trackers on some extensive sheet rock, or some such impossible pavement sort of ground.

Again, the print of a tiger can be very successfully imitated, by impressions in the sand with the two fists doubled and joined crosswise—this forms the ball of the foot; the toes are rather more a work of art to copy, though feasible—but we will not dwell on such depravity. Rather let us return to the marked down game, such animals being said to be "ringed," or surrounded, and this is the very best possible information, called in the dialect "girka khubber"—a pleasant phrase, soon learnt, and never forgotten.

The sportsman can now, at his leisure, make any arrangement he pleases or thinks best, after, of course, consulting with the leaders of his men, who, from their local and other knowledge of the particular brute's habits, can tell to a certainty almost in which direction it is likeliest to make off on being suddenly aroused from its slumbers, and so will place himself in the proper spot to ensure good clear shots at the retreating game. Meanwhile a smaller ring of beaters, who have silently climbed available trees in a circle, will have been formed round the game; this is for the double purpose of seeing exactly where it has gone, should it escape the gunners, as well as insuring its taking the proper course on being roused. This is done by driving it back when trying to quietly sneak off unobserved, by short coughing noises, or by beating two stones together (taken up the trees for the purpose), or by gently tapping the tree's trunk, or any other such slight noise, will be sufficient to turn back the animal, if made immediately in its front. After having in vain, perhaps, tried to escape by most of the guarded points, it must at length take the intended line, and so creeps on right up to where the guns are all ready in waiting. Should more than one beast be "marked down," spare men will still keep an eye on them, so that they shall not get away unseen on hearing the noise, perhaps, of killing the first roused brute. If there is any fair distance between, say a quarter of a mile or so, there will not be much chance of these also awakened animals being scared away from the neighbourhood, for though the firing will be heard plainly enough, it often happens that the echo or reverberation is so great among the surrounding hills, that it is difficult to guess from which exact quarter it comes; so to avoid running into danger, and trusting to not having been discovered, also disliking to face the great heat of sun and rocks, animals will often keep quite still in their hiding places, and so enable the sportsman to look them up in turn. Signals from the men up trees, silently made, will explain all these facts, even showing what it is, how lying down, awake or otherwise, big or little. A perfect code of signs gives every notice required. This working in concert with well-trained, willing hunters, is the great charm of all sport, and, of course, insures the biggest "bags."

In the plate a she bear is shown, with two young ones on her back—the usual mode of carrying her cubs on all occasions, until they are large enough to follow their mother safely on foot by her side, or tail rather, for she leads the way. These little brutes cling tight to the large tuft of hair between the mother's shoulders, and never fall off, even during the racing pace the old she bear sometimes makes off in. The one seen climbing the tree in the background is after honey, robbing the wild bees' nests on the outstretching branch. Bears are constantly on the look-out for this sweet food; they seem to be proof against the stings of bees, and have been described as greedily eating the bees, combs, honey, wax, and all, though I never witnessed this fact, for these robberies mostly take place at night, as a rule, when the bees have all settled, and are much confused on being so rudely awakened; yet my informants, two men of the woods, declared they had witnessed, on a fine moonlight night, the whole performance. Bears often get ugly falls from rotten boughs at this work, perhaps, for more than once, on taking off the skins of bears just shot, their bodies have been found to be covered with awful bruises, but being so very powerful, they soon recover from these accidents. They must be wonderful climbers too, for I have seen their claw-marks high up trees, far too large to be clasped or swarmed up in an ordinary manner. These same claw-marks, on all fruit trees in the jungles, are to be often observed, and from their frequency, a guess can be made as to the number of bears likely to be met with in the neighbourhood.

Bears are sometimes found in company of four or five, but mostly in pairs, or a single old one. They vary much in their behaviour; in some places charging at once in a most determined manner, without any provocation, coming on almost like a cricket ball being bowled at one. This is where they have not been much shot at, but had it all their own way with any unfortunate unarmed woodcutters, and such like defenceless people, or when the she bear has her cubs, either with her or hid in some cave close by. At other times, and far more usually, they will run off best pace on meeting with the rifleman, getting out of shot in a marvellous fashion, so it is best to be always prepared for them at any moment, by carrying your own rifle, and never trusting it in charge to another person, who may have his own safety to attend to, and forget you in the hurry.

If two or more bears are together, on one being wounded, it often turns round sharp upon the bear nearest, and commences biting and growling in the most furious manner; the other remonstrates, and the two will fight together most laughably for a few moments, when more shots from the hunter will, perhaps, help to change their thoughts into best means of escaping. This fighting with their best friends is very common, and is a most amusing sight.

This is the bear to be so often seen in camps and stations accompanying Indian jugglers; when caught very young it is easily tamed, and learns all sorts of tricks. I have seen one smoke the cocoa nut "hubble-bubble" natives use for the purpose of a pipe, eagerly. The red earth pointed mounds shown in the picture are the nests of white ants, on which bears are so fond of feeding; with their tremendous claws, they break open these high mounds, scoop out the interior part in large dry clods of baked earth, and then begin sucking at the deep holes, down which the ants and eggs are in heaps, drawing them up by force of breath.

Bears' skins make nice rugs for floors, but are hard and coarse. Dogs seem very fond of lying on these skins, for insects are seldom indeed to be found on the bear, dead or alive, perhaps from its peculiar smell, or too formidable claws. Bears are sometimes shot at by moonlight, by waiting over the caves they are known to frequent, and firing as they come out to feed—but this is poor sport.

SAMBER SHOOTING.

The deer in the foreground of this plate are the "samber stag," beautiful animals one sometimes hears miscalled the "elk." These splendid stags are far larger than the "red deer" of Scotland, standing often four feet eight inches or fourteen hands high at the shoulder, and some larger than this are found. Its body would be seven feet long, with a fine tail quite a foot in length with very wide stiff long hairs on either side. Its ears are about eight inches long and very wide. The hairs on the neck are also very long, and stiff, almost like bristles, more than half way down the neck forming a sort of ruff. The horns of the stag are very fine, spreading wide with two tines only, and being about three feet and a half long, but they vary so in shape, thickness, and length that there is no common form for them, some being most massive, but short and upright, covered with deep notches and grooves; others are very long, wide spreading, with a beautiful curve, but quite thin and smooth for the whole length; they differ also in weight materially, and so much so in appearance, that they might be mistaken for some other animal's, but the hunter will know better. The horns are dropped every year at the very beginning of the hot weather, and the new horns are not full-grown till the end of the rains, when the courting season begins. The horns are at full size after the fourth year, but continue to get larger and heavier every succeeding year for some time longer. These deer are of a dark brown colour, with a dark blueish tinge during the hot weather. The does and young fawns are of a lighter brown. All have a light yellow tinge under the tail and inside the legs. They live together in small herds of about five or six, and often in pairs, but there are far more does than stags to be seen, while a solitary old stag is often met with, far from any other herds. One stag with three does is the usual number in company. They are found in open places in the woods grazing upon the new grass blades that spring up after the jungle has been burnt, and at this time may be seen in great numbers, but not forming herds like the cheetal. They are here seen picking up the fallen fruit under trees in the early morning and cool of the evening. At other times these deer lie up close in some cool shady places; they are fond of water, but manage to exist where there is very little indeed to be found; when all the pools and rivulets have dried up during the hot weather, they then come down late in the evening to drink at some small stagnant piece of water, dirty and choked with dead leaves, but perhaps the only spot for miles round where there is a drop left not yet dried up among the hills. Over these small pools the natives watch in ambush, and many deer are killed for their valuable skins' sake, which is very soft and pliant, being also thorn proof, so is much prized and used for making shooting shoes, gaiters, covers for saddles, &c., &c.

It is easy to know where samber are to be expected in any jungles, for they have a habit of rubbing the bark off small thin low boughs, and the stems of small young trees; this is to get rid of the "velvet" that adheres to their horns in shreds up to the beginning of the "rutting season." These places are constantly to be met with in the woods and tell their own tale. Samber stags will be heard bellowing at dusk and early dawn; the noise is very loud and can be heard a good way off. They also make a short sharp kind of barking noise on being disturbed by any dangerous animal moving near their retreat, as well as on seeing men moving in the jungle; this noise always warns the sportsman either that he has been himself observed by the stag, or that some other wild beast is on the move in the vicinity, so it is as well to keep a look-out for a passing tiger, panther, &c., for they do not bark at hog or other deer, or any small harmless animals, only at foes; it is a note of warning to its friends close by.

The big stags are sometimes to be seen leaning against any slight cross grown bough, and rubbing their throats; this they will continue doing until the hair is quite worn off, and the skin quite raw for about half a foot down from a few inches below the chin; this takes place during the courting season. The does have one fawn at a time, which keeps close with the mother.

Samber can go up and down the steepest possible hills at a tremendous rate, with a great clatter of hoofs and small loose stones; they are often to be seen in single file following each other through some particular defile or pass. These runs are well known to the hill men, so when a big hunt or drive takes place by some hundred beaters turning out to work the surrounding hills for miles in one long beat, these passes are carefully manned with hunters in ambuscade. On come the startled deer at only a few paces distance, when they are easily shot; each animal being the size of a big pony, cannot well be missed, and if ever so slightly wounded is sure to be followed up and afterwards killed. "Samber's ladder" is a common native name for any inaccessible mountain path, that would puzzle a goat almost to climb. The footprint of this stag is very peculiar and not to be mistaken for any other deer; it is very long in proportion and narrow, being about two inches wide only to four inches long, the big buck's foot being easily distinguished by its far larger size, so that is the one to follow, if found alone.

Looking for samber is very pretty sport; the rifleman is in front of his men if he knows his work, otherwise he had better keep with them—two trackers will be quite enough or one even. The party proceed very slowly and of course most silently, the prints will be taken up or followed easily in most places (care of course being taken at starting to see that they are quite fresh made), but when there is any doubt or a fault, the gunner remains still, on the look-out, while the men spread a few paces on either side, intently peering on the ground for the faintest scratch, perhaps over any rocky part of ground that may be come to, and quite invisible to a novice's sight at this tracking business, or for a bent broken blade of grass even on better ground. Over burnt grass the prints can be taken at a run if needed, for the ashes resemble snow fallen an inch deep, and quite as soft, but black or grey coloured, so the least impression is plainly visible. A faint single low whistling note or hardly audible "cluck" of the tongue will inform all that the lost print has been recovered or found, when on the small party will proceed.

Sometimes while thus following up tracks, a big stag will start up and be seen perfectly motionless a few paces off, about thirty yards or so in front or perhaps a little on either side, staring hard and immoveable at the sportsmen following on its trail. These immense animals rise so silently and quickly from where they have been lying down, without any clatter of hoofs or jerking movement of the body, that to me it often seemed as if they had come up through some trap door as on the stage. The stag never moves until it perceives that it is observed, when with a spring or bound and sharp wheel off sideways, it makes off at a long cantering lumbering pace, ducking its head, horns, and neck under every low projecting bough or overhanging bush, and dodging behind each intervening clump or tree until it is out of sight in a wonderfully short time. The Bheels or men have at once spied this apparition of a stag, and have with difficulty made the raw hand at hunting aware of its presence by a silent gentle touch, perhaps on his arm, or by their earnest fixed gaze in its direction; any quick movement such as pointing with the hand would start the game, and cause it to vanish at once. When the gunner has made out this brown object through the dark gloom of the forest, he will gently and silently bring the rifle to bear on the buck's shoulder, a little behind and about half way up the breadth of its body. The smoke clears away and there is either a big kicking stag on the ground or time to give the other barrel at the stumbling faltering beast making its best efforts to escape. There is not much fear of missing a mark as big as a small horse, so close too, therefore a "kill" will be scored almost to a certainty.

Sometimes the stag's head or neck-end only will be visible as they rise in this silent manner from some low hollow spot or side of a ravine, but a shot then in the neck just under the chin will answer as well. Great care must be taken to keep clear of a big stag's horns, kicking and plunging as he will be, but the men will attend to this and hold down its head, when either the hunter can with his large "shikar knife" cut the deer's throat completely, and close up under the chin to save the skin or leather, or let the Bheels use the knife at which they are adepts. The skin round a samber's throat is very thick and tough indeed, being quite half an inch thick.

Once in my early days, as a Shikarree having upset a fine stag by a shot in the throat as described, it fell seemingly dead and motionless; while the men were coming up on my whistling, I sat down on the dead deer's flank. Suddenly and without the least warning, I found myself thrown about two yards backwards, heels up in the air—the stag had come to life again and bolted! After much astonishment we followed, when another shot killed the buck; the first bullet was found just under the skin in the throat flattened out like a half crown, and no more mischief done than merely stunning the deer for a few minutes.

Samber when in the "velvet" will lie very close, and so puzzle the hunter. Once having tracked a big buck well out into an open plain, we came upon a wide-spreading corindah bush beyond which no foot-prints were to be seen, so my men and self felt perfectly sure the stag must be somewhere close at hand. On peering under the bush nothing but what looked like a big black stone or rock was to be seen in the deep shade of the boughs, but this was the missing samber; it allowed me to fire a shot into its side at two paces distance, and then even did not move, but on giving it the other barrel it jumped up and bolted off, falling dead after going a short distance. This stag's horns had the "velvet" full upon them, were swollen to thick soft round knobs at all the points, and were very hot to touch, while they bled at many places from the scratches of the corindah sharp thorns. The animal was very thin and old; by lying so close it had hoped to deceive us, or was afraid to move, the horns in that state being so very tender. On being shot with a shell bullet, I have heard a samber scream awfully, shrieking quite loudly and unlike any other animal, for it could not run away at all.

While hunting in the "Sautpoora Range" of mountains, being obliged on some few occasions to wait patiently until very heavy clouds had passed off, I have seen on these mists clearing away samber deer all around, quite close; they seemed to come up the mountains with the clouds and then lie down, for there would be none visible before we had to wait so still; walking a few paces even would have been dangerous, for a precipice might be at one's feet, yet unseen, so dense was the white fog on these hill tops at times. Again, when shooting over the high "Barriah Mountains," and immense jungles from "Dhar" to "Dohud" station, I have seen samber lying down like cows, so very numerous and tame, often letting me get within thirty yards before rising. They were found on flat ridges at different heights as we slowly climbed up these most steep mountains, and had evidently never been hunted or fired at, for they seemed quite unconcerned as we peeped at them over the different ledges of rock in the ascent. This deer is named after the "horse stag" mentioned by Aristotle as an Indian animal, but the "nil-ghai" is thought to be really the beast intended. The horns, some very fine, are frequently found in the jungles, having been shed, and of these many are seen to have been gnawn by jackals, wild dogs, &c.

The sportsman should always carefully look over the steep sides of any hills, more or less covered with trees, bushes, large rocks or boulders fallen from above, with his pocket telescope, for often a fine stag may be so discovered lying down, with only its head and neck visible. This is a grand chance. Leave your men where they are and go yourself by making a great circuit round opposite to where the buck is resting, most carefully noting before starting any trees or conspicuous objects on the ground to be traversed to ensure your arrival at the exact spot required. After giving you plenty of time to get well above the stag, the men can rouse it from below, when it is sure to come straight up hill and pass close by where you are waiting, and so is of course killed. In this manner I have crept up very close to samber lying down near the top of a hill, as their custom is. The men can talk and smoke, as they are almost sure to do, whether prohibited or not, for this noise so engages the samber's attention, that he never looks round, but remains lying down with his large wide ears cocked well forward listening to them. Having thus once crept within twelve yards of and shot two samber through the head while still lying down, the delighted watchers were so pleased that they complimented me by saying no panther could have better stalked these deer, while getting such close shots was solely owing to the samber's whole attention being taken up with these noisy fellows left afar off in view of the game.

By wearing shooting shoes made of samber leather, without any heels or very low ones indeed, the hunter can pick his way as noiselessly as any cat. This leather is beautifully soft and pliant, and never rubs or galls the feet in the longest day's work. It is very durable and snake proof, which gives confidence in stepping through grass; moreover no thorn can pierce it. The skin of the nil-ghai is often attempted to be passed off for this truly valuable leather, but is easily detected.

While on the subject of deer, the "hog deer" may be mentioned, although this animal is chiefly to be found in "Sindh," where it is common enough on the banks of rivers and ravines covered with the shady "jhow" or tamarisk bushes, also called the "bastard cypress," and in patches of high grass, where they lie close hidden during the daytime, and are driven out by beaters past the marksmen in ambush. There are some few hog deer in Central India, but I have never met any there, though it is common on the Bengal side or Presidency, also in Burmah. This deer is about two feet three inches high, and from snout to tail would be four feet three inches, of which the tail is eight inches long, rather bushy and white underneath. The hair is long and coarse, quite bristly on the back and neck, and there really is a good deal of the pig's shape in its rounded back and low way of carrying the head. The colour is a dark brown, but gets lighter in the hot weather; there are a few rows of white spots along the back and flanks, like the "cheetal." The horns also resemble the cheetal's, but are much smaller. These deer do not herd together, but are started singly or two or three at most. The young ones are very much spotted, and of a far lighter brown colour. The does are without horns. When a griffin one of these bucks gave me an ugly prod in the thigh with its horn.

Another small deer which I have only met with in "Rajpootana," though it is also found in Southern India, is the "four-horned antelope." These animals would jump up quite close, while walking through any thick bushy jungle, mostly on the sides of hills, and used to go off in a succession of bounding leaps, that made it very difficult to hit them with a ball, but a few were shot now and then for the pot, being good eating. They were of a dark brown colour, with light dirty white inside the legs and stomach, also inside the ears, with whitish ring marks on the legs. They stood about two feet high at the shoulder, which was very low; they had two sets of horns, the upper ones only about five inches long, upright and quite smooth (like miniature blue bull horns), the lower pair were very short, mere stumps about an inch and a half long, all four black and smooth, very curious to view. These deer soon get out of sight after a few bounds, they would run with their necks stretched out and held very low down, dodging among the bushes and rocks, so one had to be very quick for a shot. It was one of the so-called "wild sheep" of the natives.

Once, and only once, while shooting bears with a friend in the "Dhang," a dense almost unexplored forest jungle in Western Khandeish, I saw what must have been an "ibex" or "neelghery wild goat." We had been very lucky with the bears, getting eight in three days, and wounding three others, for they were plentiful, being attracted to some very high mountains at "Mooleir" by a large wild sort of root then ripe. The Bheels had marked down four more bears, and we were slowly climbing a very precipitous hill, when about half way up, they called out to us from above, having started an animal at the top, which came straight down this awful cliff in long jumps of quite ten yards at a time, with its hind legs tucked up close under its body, with a shower of small stones following in its course, displaced by its feet at each drop; when just opposite us and not more than thirty paces off it stopped dead short, all four feet in a point together, and looked round. It appeared of a reddish brown colour and looked as big as a small donkey, its short thick flat horns curved quite round in a circle, with numerous rings on them, were distinctly visible. I had just brought my rifle to bear upon it, when my friend, reminding me that we were after bears, touched my arm—a great mistake this to any one about to fire and dangerous in the extreme. The "ibex" gave a hasty glance at us, then pitched himself head foremost down the rest of the precipice at a frantic pace. We could see him for more than half a mile, descending until he got lost in the thick jungle below. This chance was so lost, worth any fifty bears! I went back alone but could not again find the strange animal. On describing this beast and showing a drawing made at once from memory to some old sportsmen they told me they had also seen something of the sort years before when employed with troops in that part of the country, but did not know what it was, and the Bheels seemed to think it rare. This lost opportunity will never be forgotten, for no other such animal ever again presented itself.

There is a kind of "wild sheep" to be found in the "Hala Mountains," near Kurrachee, called "ghud," that is driven past hunters in ambush in small herds. This animal is peculiar to Scinde, Beloochistan or Persia. Another small deer that will be frequently met with in the woods is the "rib faced or barking deer," commonly called the "beekree" or wild sheep, also the "ravine deer." It is of a bright reddish brown colour, with white inside the legs, under the tail and behind, also the chin, with white spots on all four legs, and dark brown marks down the face. Those found in Rajpootana were of a more sandy or lighter colour than elsewhere. This deer stands about two feet three inches high, very low in the shoulder; it has rather a long tail of wide bristly hairs. The horns are about nine inches long with one small tine, and the tips curved back most curiously. The doe has no horns, but tufts of black stiff hair on small bony knobs instead; she is smaller than the buck. These little deer are very good eating, so after a day's sport they are always looked for on the way home, as they make a grand addition to the pot, for from always living in shady places they are not baked by the sun, so their flesh does not become tasteless, like most Indian game, but is really good venison. They are generally to be found amongst grass-grown ravines. On coming near where one may be hiding in low bushy jungle, a loud sharp bark will be heard, repeated at intervals; this noise it makes on being disturbed or surprised by any passing object. Now keep quite still, when the small deer will presently show itself, moving in a few short bounds or quick sort of trot for a few yards, and then stopping to look round and listen. A whistle will often make it discover itself by moving forward its large wide red ears, as it stands almost hidden from view in the high grass. A close shot can mostly be had at about fifty yards or so, but it requires to be fairly hit or will creep off through thick tangled bushes in an extraordinary manner and be lost, although lots of blood may be about. In the very early morning and evening they come out into open spaces to graze; only one is to be generally seen, and not more than two at any time near each other, though by beating a long strip of narrow jungle, I have seen half a dozen so collected and driven past separately.

The natives say these deer are a good deal chased by the wild dogs, and I have been solemnly told that the buck, when so pursued, will leap up and hook himself on by the curved tips of his horns to any moderately high cross bough that may be in the way, and so manage to baffle the hounds by twisting his body up in a ball shape, while the dogs, busy below in trying to recover the lost scent, never think of looking up! This method of eluding pursuit may be all very well for the buck, but the doe without horns would be caught, an objection that would be replied to by a silent shrug of the shoulders, and certainly stop any further information.

These little deer are often heard barking during the night, no doubt being disturbed by some prowling beast. When trotting off briskly it sometimes makes a clattering noise with its feet like castanets. During the rains, when the flies drive every animal clear of the jungles, this small deer will be found out in the open plains, but always where there is high grass and on the borders of forest ground.

One more tiny deer remains to be described that will occasionally come under the hunter's notice, viz., the "mouse deer" or "pisai" of the natives. It is only about a foot high and twice as long, weighing about five and a half pounds, or as much as a big hare (Indian). It is of a dirty yellow grey colour, white underneath, with long rows of spots like bars lengthways on the sides, and has large brown ears. It is mostly to be met with in the forests of Southern India, but is also found in Central India. This tiny deer is very shy and rarely to be seen moving about, but they sometimes start up quite close to one's feet, and rush off into some thick bush not far off, and there try to hide by lying very close indeed. I have known them to get under dry dead heaps of fallen bamboo clumps, and though touched roughly with a stick, would not even then move out. They move about chiefly at night, and the tiny footprints may be seen along paths in the jungles, a mere letter V shape split at the point, for it treads on the very tips of its toes; they frequent hard stony ground, and these prints show where the deer have gone to and fro for water. They are so small and the animal is so seldom seen, that at first one wonders what can have made such minute footsteps. A snap shot with a charge of big shot from a gun is best to procure a specimen. The skin makes a table mat.

CHAPTER VII.

BISON SHOOTING.

Description of the Indian Wild Bull and his Habits—Hunting Lodges—The Stalk—Fatal Shots—An Attempted Charge—Bison Tricks—Tigers and Wounded Bull—Gigantic Silk Moths—Monkeys—Snakes—Wolverine—Jungle Fowl—Elephants—A Phantom Bison—Nature's Spies—A Ride among Wild Cattle—Firearms.

(*Plate IX. depicts the grand Indian Wild Bull, generally described in England as the Bison.*)

This chapter introduces the hunter to the largest of all Indian game, barring the elephant and rhinoceros, viz. :—the "gaur," or "jungli khulga" of the natives, and "bison" of the English in India—a sad misnomer, for by this term, an animal, something like the American buffalo, is generally understood by people at home; whereas this grand "Indian wild bull" would make about two of such imposters, as the following dimensions of a fine bull, but nothing extraordinary, taken most carefully by myself, with a measuring tape, very shortly after it was shot, at Mundoorlee, in the "Dandille Jungles," on 30th April, 1870, will show :—

	ft.	in.
Height from shoulder to toe	6	2
Length, from nose to tip of tail . . .	12	10
Girth, at widest, over hump	9	4
From nose, between horns, or length of head altogether	2	3
Round neck at widest	7	0

	ft.	in.
Round fore arm at widest	2	1½
Round hind leg at widest	2	11
Round hough	1	9

Other dimensions of horns I have by me show as follows:—

	ft.	in.
Girth of horns round base	1	8½
Length of horn, outside curve	2	3½
Spread between tips of horns	2	2¼
Widest spread from outside horns . . .	3	0½
Breadth of forehead, between eyes . . .	1	1½

So much for measurements, which, at the best, give but vague ideas. The average height of these splendid cattle may be set down at quite six feet, and rather more than stout in proportion, for they are anything but lean kine, being most massive at all points, so much so, that one would prove a tight fit for an ordinary parlour door. They are of a very dark brown colour, so dark, that at a litle distance the bulls look black. The cows are of a lighter brown, and the calves lighter still—just the colour of samber deer. The bison's legs, from below the knees and houghs, are of a pure white, most conspicuous. The head is most massive, with a ridge of solid bone in the middle, from which the horns spring on either side, borne high on the forehead, and spreading out in a half-moon shape, the points of some old bulls' horns being wide asunder, while others have their tips curved in much closer. These horns, in the case of old bulls, are much notched, and have slight rings, or broken half curves rather, at the base; while the points of some such horns are quite broken off, or worn down and splintered, the middle part of the horn is smooth. The cows' horns are much smaller and smoother, and rather curve backwards at the tips. The calves have merely little black stumps for horns, according to their size and age. The horns of the young bulls are not so massive and formidable looking, but smoother, and very graceful. These horns take a fine polish, and make pretty stands for flowers, when fitted up with cross silver wire covers, and filled as cornucopias, &c., while the spread of a bison's skull and horns is a great ornament in halls.

The newly-severed head and horns of a big bull are a good weight to raise up a foot high off the ground, with both hands even. The hair just over the bison's eyes is of a light reddish colour, and curly. The muzzle is flesh colour. The eyes are light blue. The ears are wide, and groved inside, of a light, dirty brown tint. The neck is most massive, and the skin thicker there than at any other part of the body, being quite from one-and-a-half to two inches thick, and really bullet-proof for the old light charges of rifles. Along the back rises a most curious ridge, like the keel of a boat, which ends half-way down the back, rather abruptly, starting from the great round but low shoulder hump. There is some loose skin, something like a dewlap, hanging down from the throat, but not deep. The bison's body seems to fall off a little towards the hind quarters; but the hind legs, like the fore arms, are most full and powerful. Inside the thighs and arms and under the stomach, the hair is rather curly, and of a yellow reddish tinge. The rest of the coat is short, very close lying, dark brown hair, and there is a peculiar smell about the whole animal, like fresh herbs or thyme. The tail is about a yard long, thin and bony towards the end, with a bunch of long hair or tuft, like any other cattle. The hoofs, for so large a beast, are very small—of a deer-like shape, with a truly game look, and they are most sure-footed on them, running full pace round the edge of a precipice, and so steep that only one outer half of the hoof-mark has been shown when following these prints—a mere succession of single curved marks on hard, rocky ground too—the sort of place where the hunter is glad to hold on by his hands to every passing clump to save himself from going over some frightful cliff.

The cows are easily distinguished from the bulls, being smaller, and of a far lighter build, without the low round hump, and with legs or stockings of even a purer white, while their footprints, with a little practice, can be recognized so that one need not follow their marks by mistake for a bull's. On seeing the herd together, the greater size and darker colour of the bulls at once point them out.

The great charm of bison shooting consists in the fact of its requiring the very perfection of stalking to ensure even the most moderate success. The sharp look-out that has to be kept up from the moment of finding a set of prints that show by their size that the maker or owner will be well worth following up, for his splendid head and horns, the prize sought for, will certainly be in proportion or correspond with the trail. The utter uncertainty of the length of the coming chase, for the first glimpse of the monstrous game will be sure to be most unexpected, no matter whether the animal is stumbled upon after going a few hundred yards only in pursuit, or after a whole day's fag, or with, perhaps, the dreadful disappointment of not being able to come in view at all, with all your labour thrown away, or with the quite as bad alternative of your having by some neglect or carelessness, allowed the bison to outwit you, when a snort and clattering of hoofs, far out of harm's way, will convince you of having several lessons yet to learn in the art of circumventing such a shy, knowing, vigilant beast; the great necessity for being prepared to act at any half moment's notice; and lastly, a certain undefined sense that you had better be careful for your own sake.

These are some of the delights of this particular chase,

during which the hours will have slipped by altogether unheeded. Added to all is the charm of the lovely scenery passed through, and which must impress itself most forcibly, in spite of the attention being so engrossed with the tracking and bright look-out duties.

Again, as one always likes to have some excuse for committing murder, you think of the excellence of the beef, the number of hands it will feed, the usefulness of the skin—for this is greatly prized by natives to cut into long thongs, with which they bind up their carts and different farming implements—the mischief to these cultivators' crops the bison causes, and that you are helping to rid the neighbourhood of a dangerous nuisance; for there is little doubt that a herd of these brutes will now and then help to clear off a field of grain in a single night, and that they are not to be driven off when so engaged; also, that a single savage old bull expelled the herd, or leading a solitary life from choice, will sometimes take up his quarters near an outlying village, and make it warm indeed for any one passing by his hiding place, charging, without provocation, labourers going to their work in the ealy dawn, when they are either tossed, gored, or escape by a miracle. From these causes many a small, rising village, or newly-planted colony in the forest depths, has been deserted in despair. Otherwise, the bison are harmless enough, grazing on the endless supply of jungle grass, or browsing on the young green shoots of the bamboo, and keeping far from the haunts of men; they would never be disturbed, by natives at least, who consider them sacred as the common cow, or so closely related to it, that they deserve the same protection, if not worship, exactly.

Herds of bison are sometimes to be seen quite fifty or more together, grazing their way through the high grass jungle, a little apart from each other, but feeding in the same direction, and keeping in one body, at the very early morning.

Again, only about a dozen or so will be met with, or perhaps only four or five, with a big black bull to about every ten cows, or less, while two bulls, or a single one, will be found living by themselves, away from the herd for a time. These cattle have been grazing all night from the previous evening, so directly the sun begins to get warm, they think about lying up during the great heat of the day in some cool, shady spot, either getting down into the beds of deep ravines, or nullahs densely grown with young green bamboo trees, or high dry grass, or else creeping under the shady overspreading boughs of several jungle trees, close growing together, and so matted overhead with creepers that scarcely a speck of daylight is to be anywhere seen peeping through. Or in the case of a single big bull, he will be found to have betaken himself to the extreme top of some most steep, high hill, after having laid in a supply of water enough to last for the day, previous to commencing his mountainous ascent. Here, under some shady overhanging tree, or behind some dense clump of bamboos, he will lie chewing the cud, and half asleep, mostly on the very edge of some precipice, up which the cool winds blow most soothingly, and quite strong enough to drive off any pests of flies, gnats, &c., with the most charming scenery spread out below for his contemplation, miles upon miles away till lost in space.

Besides being such a watchful timid animal, ready to start off headlong at the faintest sound or glimpse of the hunter, bison are often to be found in company with samber and wild hog; these animals act as sentinals or scouts to the herd, and afford additional protection. They are supposed to seek the bison's company as some safeguard from the tiger, but it may be merely accidental association after all, though the rifleman will find it extra difficult to surprise any particular member of such a family party.

A hunting trip after bison having been arranged, we will

now suppose that the sportsmen—two are enough, but of course more could join—have reached the particular part of the vast forest they intend working over. The reason for naming so few guns, is the great difficulty, from the extreme scarcity of men in these jungles, of procuring enough from the different far scattered villages to act as porters in carrying the very reduced allowance of baggage each hunter has to content himself with during these expeditions. Another point is that by each taking widely different directions on starting for each day's hunt, they are not so likely to disturb each other's sport, either by accidentally following up the same set of footprints or by scaring away each other's game by gun shots, heard close by just perhaps at a most critical moment. It would be very little use for the two to work together, for they would be sure to interfere unintentionally enough with each other's chance, it being hard enough for one gun to sufficiently conceal himself at times. A deserted hut or shed formed of bamboos cut down and tied together with the roof covered over with heaps of dry grass, leaves, boughs, &c., has been found. This extremely rude shelter has been either run up by some former party of hunters, or a new one has to be built on any well-selected spot, where good water and plenty of it is forthcoming, by all hands turning to with a will, and by means of their short axes or bill hooked shaped knives, clearing the ground and cutting down the required number of bamboo poles: these are tied together with bark strips or interlaced, and from long practice a really delightful bower is constructed in a wonderfully expeditious manner, most useful for keeping the sportsmen's kit in, as well as affording perfect shelter from the sun or sudden violent storms, perfect hurricanes that sometimes break most unexpectedly over the forests.

Very little is to be done on arriving at new ground in this manner beyond making the hut comfortable and complete, getting dinner ready, and hearing from any local villagers all the news regarding the chance of sport in the neighbourhood. This last is often a most pumping business, for these people wisely decline to commit themselves, lest on their being taken out as guides the next morning, no game may be forthcoming. However, after a little talk carried on in a quiet coaxing manner, and admissions that of course you do not expect to find any wild animals tied up with a rope in particular spots, which is the usual formula for explaining that you are well aware of the uncertain habits of all kinds of game, it will be generally admitted by degrees that such and such wild beasts may be looked for. Promises of liberal reward will make these statements more positive than mere hints or suppositions, so the sportsmen turn in for the night cheered with the almost certainty of next day's sport.

Rising before daylight so as to be ready at the first streak of dawn for a start, for day breaks and is followed by broad light with very little delay, the hunter sets out with his one or two steady native companions, who act as trackers, guides in the pathless woods (to be lost in which is far beyond a joke), and carriers of the water bag, ("chagul"), spare ammunition, and food for the party of three. The small leather water bag, in which about two quarts of deliciously cool water can be carried—for the leather being porous the hot wind blowing on the bag acts as a refrigerator—can be left behind or not according to the chances of finding plenty of water fit to drink in the jungles. At a pinch for water, the long green creeper called "bale" which hangs in festoons from tree branches, and which resembles hollow piping about an inch thick, can be cut, when a small supply of dew water will be obtained, but the plant is not always to be met with when wanted.

On first setting out, the long grass one has to walk through or which overhangs the narrow side paths selected, will be found saturated with last night's dew, so that a very few steps will wet the sportsman to the middle, while every bamboo clump he passes under is in a like condition, so that a regular shower bath greets him from above on accidentally touching any wide-spreading twigs. These little annoyances are nothing and do not last long, for directly the sun has once risen he will be dry enough for the rest of the day, while the chances are that where the wet dew has been brushed aside in long tracks, the course taken by some big animal during the night in its latest wanderings will be clearly shown. Silently following these traces until some open clear ground will admit of these footsteps being examined, and congratulating himself on so soon having got some clue, the hunter and his guides, all with their eyes open to full stretch—for who can tell how soon the game, whatever it may be, will be overtaken?—continue to take up the fresh prints until some open soft spot shows plainly the sort of animal in whose tracks they have been wandering. A big boar or samber deer, neither of these requires another thought. The first is unshootable, the second can be fired at or not if met with on the return home. A cow bison perhaps with a calf at its heels, or two or more cows. These are only considered on the speculation that they may lead to the rest of the herd to which they belong and have become separated from for the time, or perhaps show where they have taken their last drink of water before retiring for the day's shelter and rest. But only suppose it should be a big bull, he will be at once followed up, or if perhaps thought not quite worthy, the party will proceed, taking their chance of coming in the course of a mile or so across country upon some perfect monster's prints, when the chase will begin in earnest, great care being of course taken to see that the trail is perfectly fresh; very little doubt can exist on this point so early in the morning, for the fresh perfectly dry earth will be seen removed at each step, showing much lighter in colour than the rest of the untrodden ground still damp with dew.

The tracking of such a large heavy animal is of course simple enough, except perhaps where it may have crossed over some stony places, such as "sheet-rock," which will extend at times for a hundred yards or so as smooth as pavement, but in irregular layers, or else where fallen leaves from the "teak" trees may be lying in patches of about thirty yards wide, quite knee-deep, and rustling to a most provoking degree, for these leaves are dry as tinder and each as large as rhubarb leaves, and on being trodden on make a noise that has not inaptly been compared to walking on tin boxes! So these loud noisy spots are at once avoided, a circuit round them being made, one man opening out and so each taking a half side; the trail will be hit off somewhere in advance, when all can jog on as before. But should any doubt arise or other tracks have crossed the line taken, it may be necessary to begin at where the teak leaves first caused all traces to be lost, when by carefully removing a few of the top or latest fallen leaves, the sharp points of the bull's hoofs will be seen dug deep into the decaying mass of vegetation below; these will point out the true course and land you on the open ground beyond free from doubt.

All this may seem to be most unnecessary trouble, but it is far better than losing a really good trail, or following up by mistake one that will only bring you on a wretched cow at last. In this manner the party will proceed at what is necessarily a somewhat slow rate, keeping the brightest possible look-out well ahead and on all sides for a view of the expected game. Stooping low down and carefully peering all round on coming to the top of any rising ground that may afford a more extended view of the glades beyond, and listening most attentively for any sound—for in passing decayed clumps of bamboo or in browsing on the young green shoots of the same long canes, a slight crashing noise may be heard, which will betray the bison's presence—carefully noticing these same so lately broken and still wet chewed twigs, as well as any other signs that by their freshness may give an idea of how short a time may have elapsed since they were dropped, the hunters will now have gone a considerable distance. Perhaps a short quick call, like a single note from a bugle, may have been heard, repeated two or three times only; this will give warning that bison, though perhaps not the one pursued, are ahead and signalling their missing scattered friends. Now the trail will be found to become less direct, more wandering from side to side in any direction with marks of where a halt has taken place at short intervals.

These are signs that the game will soon be come up with; extra caution and silence are now observed, when at length on peering over the highest ridge of some broken rising ground, the long-sought bull will be seen some sixty yards or more just ahead, walking at a most leisurely pace and looking undecidedly from side to side; you won't get a better chance, so when his flank is a little broadside on in his wandering, fire at the bison's side, one third of the depth of his body from, and in a perpendicular line to, the end of the ridge on his back, taking care of course not to shoot too far behind if he is moving. This shot will break his liver and flatten itself against the inside skin beyond. There is nothing more to be done but keep him well in sight and wait the result. A mighty rush forward will follow the shot's "thud," for a few hundred yards at a terrific pace; this will soon slacken into a stately walk, and then the bull will either slowly lie down or try to prop himself against some clump of bamboo on passing, to be quickly followed by much cracking of the same, as he staggers to and fro for a minute and then rolls over dead, having bled to death internally, choked with blood.

All this will take about five minutes from the shot being fired. Now walk up safely enough and admire the prize. The horns can be cut out with the men's axes, together with the high bony crest that connects them, and this will be found quite sufficient load, to be changed in turns as it is carried back to the encamping ground or small hut on the men's heads, or borne between them on a pole on their shoulders. This liver shot in particular is named as the best at any distant animal. It never kills at once or at all affects any brute's charging or fighting powers for about five minutes afterwards; still it is the most certain killing of all shots, and one that merely gives the trouble of a short "following up."

When new to bison shooting I lost several fine bulls by trying for a shot below the shoulder or much too forward, some tradition existing that the fatal shot was either there or in the neck high up. These animals all got off, even after being followed for miles, when remembering how well this liver shot told with every other brute, I tried it, with invariable success ever afterwards.

Referring to my journal and notes during a period in all of four months' shooting in these jungles, extending over three successive seasons, sixty-six bison were blazed at, the largest bulls being always selected, though at first a poor cow or two suffered by mistake, having been too hastily pointed out as fair game by the trackers, who were most desirous of tasting beef with as little danger or delay as possible, but this error was soon corrected, never to occur again. For a close standing shot sideways on, I should try at the neck just where the head joins, rather high up or about six inches below the nape of the neck. An instant upset will mostly follow this shot, but not always. For a front standing shot, rake the animal well centre in the chest—not throat, remember, but low down. The head being held so high and well thrown back affords no safe front shot. The shot just behind or under the shoulder to pierce the lungs seldom answers.

Talking of the beef, twice I have tasted bison veal; nothing could be more delicious or tender. A friend's shots having missed some running cattle, by accident upset these calves, or the balls may have glanced. The big bull's steaks are very good, but liable to be tough meat, though hunter's appetite will not mind that little drawback; plenty of mustard should be used. One feels quite ravenous over this change of diet.

I have several times at immense trouble skinned bulls, deemed worthy specimens, and borne the skin, with horns, hoofs, all complete, to the temporary shed or camping place, and there with no less trouble, after pegging down and stretching the immense hide, employing for the purpose quite five hundred bamboo pegs—a hole to receive the horns having been previously dug in the earth—and finally after rubbing in arsenical soap by the pailful, have felt certain that a most perfect trophy had at last been secured, from which others strangers to the animal except by name, might be able to judge of its mighty size, only to find that all this bother and precaution had been in vain, for these skins would be sure to be taken up (of course by mistake) too soon, and so found to be full of maggots and spoilt, or else the heavy rain had soaked them till sodden, when again the maggots would appear and corrupt the whole skin. These vexatious accidents took place so often that the attempt had to be given up and only the horns secured, but knowing how the skin is valued by the natives, I have always felt sure that a good deal of method was used in so spoiling these specimen skins during my absence while looking for more or travelling on a few miles to fresh hunting grounds.

The meat of the just killed bison would not be wasted, for long before vultures, jackals, &c., could do any harm to it, the villages around would have sent men, women, and children to the spot on hearing the news. These would remove the green boughs with which it is always best to cover up at once any fresh-killed bull, to prevent as much as possible the effects of the sun tainting the meat, flies swarming over it, &c. These people all sitting down close to the carcase, a grand feast would be held, lasting all night and longer, if more bison happened to be killed pretty close to each other, as would sometimes occur. Something stronger than water would be drunk at these feasts to assist digestion, but this is supposition only.

Here may be mentioned that the bison has thirteen pairs of ribs, the "aurochs" or European wild bulls have fourteen pairs, and the American buffalo or bison fifteen pairs, a marked difference in the several animals. The other Indian tame cattle have all thirteen pairs of ribs, showing the bison's claim to be considered a true "wild bull," but it is too late to alter the name, though hunters mostly use the right term, "khulga," when talking among themselves.

This last description of a stalk after bison was merely the ordinary state of things, for of course these chases vary endlessly and not always harmlessly to all concerned. The country where bison are found is always so very extensive, that driving them towards gunners posted at likely runs must be very uncertain work; still it is attempted in certain places. These wild cattle unless mortally wounded can carry off any amount of lead, but of course to die soon afterwards. The shot in the side has been named as the most effective, but ideas vary on this point. Once getting a fair front perfectly still shot at a bull's head as he gazed at me at about eighty paces off over the top of some bushes and young green bamboo jungle, the bison dropped at once to the shot aimed exactly between the eyes, and just below the bony crest which carries the massive horns. On going up close, the bull suddenly jumped up within a few paces, and was racing off when two more shots were fired into its hind quarters, all that was visible through the closing bushes; this was to ensure getting plenty of blood for following-up purposes. Where the bull had fallen we picked up a long warm plug of white fat-looking stuff as big as one's thumb. This appeared to be brain, but though that beast was followed up for quite four miles it was never seen again. The ball no doubt had punched out this piece of brain, yet beyond upsetting him temporarily no great harm seemed to have been caused the bison by such a wound.

After this experience I did not try much for a head shot, except once to dodge round and round a big bull that had been rolled over and seemed pinned to the ground by a shot through the neck. This bison had kicked a clear wide open space for about four yards all round where he fell among low bushes, and continued so kicking with his heels lashing out quite five feet high for more than five minutes after being hit, and would have gone on doing so, his eyes starting out of their sockets and much snorting, until a shot behind the crest at the back of the skull quieted him for good; it was most puzzling where to fire, for I expected he would rise up at every moment and be mischievous. Another lucky neck shot fired at a venture once secured a grand old bull. After taking some prints many miles, and at last creeping on all fours among some "carwar" bushes (the Jerusalem artichoke sort of stalks and leaves previously mentioned), something black was seen to be lying down about thirty yards ahead. Leaving the two men, I crawled on for another twenty yards, but even then only a round black mark as big as the top of a hat could be seen. It was of little use firing at this, which might have been the animal's hind quarters, and so invulnerable almost; but after waiting a little while and going through a perfect pantomime with the men behind, who wished to know what part of the beast was visible, a gentle regular continued movement about a yard to the right of this black round mass could be faintly seen; this after much thought I concluded must be the bull's lower jaw engaged in chewing the cud, so aiming at an angle where the neck ought to be, bang went the rifle and all was still; the bull had been shot dead just where the head joins on, high up at the back of the neck, no doubt dislocated, a perfect accident, for nothing visible was aimed at.

Another lucky shot was made at a monster bull as he was making off at a long trot, having either winded or perceived us on his trail. Thinking he was as good as lost almost, I fired at two hundred yards for the sake of getting some blood to follow up on. There was a vicious kick out behind, and the "thud" noise plainly audible, but no blood to be found, so the tracking was continued up an almost perpendicular hill, so steep that one's hands had to be often used, for bison will crawl up anywhere. Just as we got up to the top and peeped over the edge, the man with me pointed to the bison lying down; it gave a tremendous snort on catching sight of us and was rising up, rather slowly it seemed, when I gave him both barrels in the neck at about twenty-five yards distance; he now stood up, and after banging his horns against a tree close by, stamping his fore feet and swinging his body to and fro, gave a shrill loud whistle sort of scream, like an engine leaving a railway station, and came on best pace; but meanwhile fresh cartridges had been got ready, so jumping aside and behind a friendly tree, I fired as he passed into his ribs at two yards distance barely; this luckily rolled him down the steep hill side, with much smashing of trees, bamboo clumps, and rolling of loose stones. Here we soon after came upon him dead, but with one hind leg broken at the hough, clean and dangling; this was the first lucky long shot, but though it did not cause the blood to show or stop in the least his climbing powers, no doubt it impeded what was meant for his charging pace, as well as rising up, for these brutes are on their legs like lightning at any alarm, springing up from their beds in high green grass and bolting off at an inconceivable rate of swiftness for their great size.

Sometimes on coming upon these pressed-down grass beds, showing the animal's whole form most completely, I have been reminded by the warm scent of a cow-house door thrown suddenly open, so strongly would the perfect cow-like smell of the late occupants be left in the surrounding high grass or reeds. The faintest noise or the slightest sniff of the hunter is sufficient to set a large herd of bison scampering off down the steepest hills at headlong pace, the clatter they make in so doing giving me for the first time the idea that part of the opposite side of the mountain had suddenly slipped and was rolling down bodily! The smashing of bamboos and trees caused by such a number of heavy animals is something astonishing to listen to, stones too follow rolling down after them. The herd will not pull up after a flight of this kind till well at the bottom of some tremendous mountain or "ghauts," and far away hid in the densest jungle; for this reason great care should be taken in every stalk after a distant bull that may have been luckily spied, to approach him from windward, or the chances of surprising the game are almost nil.

Plate IX. shows how a monster bull has been tracked to his place of repose, where in a half-dozing dreamy state of mind he is chewing the cud lazily, and enjoying the stiff cool breeze that blows up the side of the mountain, assuring freedom from all annoyance of flies, gnats, &c., while a slight shady tree overhead acts as an umbrella or sun-shade. He chooses the black rocky ground to lie on as corresponding to his own coat, and thus rendering him less conspicuous. Bison are quite aware of the advantage of such a back-ground, and are often to be found amongst large boulder rocks exactly their own colour, or else standing close by some large decayed tree that appears quite charcoal colour, having been burnt and charred high up by successive jungle fires, that occur mostly once a year, when the long grass is set alight by the herdsmen to ensure a new crop of grass springing up for their cattle to

Maj. Gen. W. Rice, Delt. Shaw & Sons, Lith.

A HERD OF INDIAN BISON _ "GAUR" OR "KHULGA"

feed on; or the fire may have been caused by lightning, or by boughs dry as tinder being ignited by friction caused by the wind, or from the ashes of some native's pipe; so it is not an unknown occurrence, in the uncertain light or gloom of the forest, for one of these burnt tree stumps to be fired into by mistake for some part of the half-hidden bison's body. I once so blazed into a large burnt fallen tree trunk, behind which a bull was lying down, with only the top of his head and horns visible above the log in the very early grey twilight of dawn, and was much surprised and vexed on being recalled by the men from a race after the supposed wounded bull, at being shown the bullet deeply and harmlessly lodged in this charred mass of fallen timber.

The white heap of foam, like a lady's lace pocket-handkerchief, just under the bull's nose, is the result of his cud-chewing amusement, or habit. The green, wide leaves worn by the trackers are twined round their heads for coolness sake, also to render them less visible, when just peeping over the top or side of some large rock, or from behind any tree-trunk, or such like post of advantage for a view ahead, themselves unseen. Some doubt whether a mere barely to be observed scratch on the black sheet-rock is caused by the foot of the missing bull, or is the mark of some other wandering animal—buck samber, perhaps—has caused a silent consultation to be held of hunter and men. The big birds flying overhead are "toucans." These most curious-looking birds are frequently to be seen and heard in these jungles; their call is most peculiar, like the chattering of gigantic magpies, and at its sound all the snake tribe are said by the natives to hide their heads, for some cause unexplained. These fine birds are great fruit eaters, living on the ripe "jack" fruit—a large, strong-smelling coarse fruit, with a very rough, green skin—quite two feet in length, and half as thick, very plentiful in places, and much prized by bears also as food—men, too, eat it. The curious high crown, and immense long, thick bills of these birds are very light indeed, and soon perish when dried; for I once shot a pair of these toucans as specimens, but the insects soon destroyed the bills and crowns, by boring minute holes in them. "Hornbill" is another common name for these birds.

This old bull in question will now soon be discovered, and either left quivering on the spot by a shot just behind the ear, or be sent off with a rush from a ball in his flank, a foot below the ridge of his back, which will rake him through for a yard, or more, internally, and bring on violent fits of coughing—to be heard from afar, causing him to tumble over dead in a few minutes. If left dead, his horns will be cut out—a troublesome job—while the hunter will take a short rest under the large shady tree, after having taken the bull's measurements, or even a hasty sketch of the defunct monster. The "chagal," or leather water-bottle, will help dilute some whiskey—drank painfully weak, to the health of the next big bull to be found.

The bright red "squirrel," overhead in the tree, is a very pretty little animal, but certainly more than twice as large as an English squirrel. They are very common in the vast jungles of Southern India, and are constantly heard calling—a most peculiar cry, that has been well compared to the running-down of a large eight-day clock. These very pretty squirrels are easily tamed, when caught young, and make nice pets.

While one is roaming through these vast forests, extending for several hundred miles in length, by about fifty miles in breadth, bison will be sometimes stumbled upon most unexpectedly. Once, while following a small, narrow path, a big bull walked out of a patch of thick bamboo jungle, a few yards only just before me. A couple of shots, instantly fired at his neck and flank, sent him off at racing pace. Quickly shoving in fresh cartridges, I gave chase, diving into the thick bushes headlong, where the retreating bull had disappeared, hoping to get more shots at the bolting game, when I almost ran up against this bison, full tilt, for it had pulled up suddenly. It was so dark among these tall, dense bushes, that I did not see him until within touching distance. With difficulty stopping myself while running my fastest, I pulled both triggers, firing from the hip, when over went the bull, like so many yards of black park paling blown down—the powder, no doubt, helping to upset him as much as the two bullets. Luckily he did not rise again, but died there, kicking tremendously.

Too great caution cannot be used in thus giving chase to wounded bison, for they have a nasty trick of suddenly wheeling round in their flight behind any thick clump of bamboo or other bushes in passing, and there standing quite still and motionless. After thus running a short course, in the shape of the letter J, up comes the hunter, fully convinced the bull is straight on before him, when, on getting opposite, or passing the bison so concealed in waiting on one side, out rushes the brute, full tilt, when nothing but a miracle saves one from being tossed or knocked over, and hurt most severely.

Having once wounded two bulls out of a herd, I was giving chase in this manner, when one of the bulls was to be heard groaning, and making a great kicking noise in a small ravine a few yards in front, down which he seemed to have tumbled; cautiously looking ahead, and trying to peep down the sloping bank, suddenly the two men following behind me, began to give the loud, shrill whistle, quickly repeated, that denotes something dangerous being close at hand. Thinking they only referred to the fallen bull just in front, and wished to warn me of what I might not be aware,

I still walked on, when the whistles again, so sharply repeated, made me look round, when there, to my horror, was the second wounded bull just behind me, striking, with his fore leg raised up, far higher than my head (just as a very young colt does in play). I swung round, and luckily dropped the bull by giving him both barrels, fired from my hip, close into his chest. This brute had come on so silently behind, I never even heard him, being so engaged looking down for the dying bison in front in the low sloping ravine. This second bull was, no doubt, too much hurt to get up a charge, or he could have pitched me a long way off. It had let me pass close while hiding behind a big bush. These two bison were left dead within fifty paces of each other; and on shortly afterwards going in that direction, their skins were to be seen hung upon a long pole each, like carpets on lines, as the custom is with natives, who thus leave the skins, too heavy to move, to dry in the open air, till fit to be cut up into thongs, than which no rope can be stronger or more lasting.

Again, when once following up a wounded bull late in the evening, after going many miles, for the beast kept moving just ahead, but could not be clearly viewed for another shot, three tigers were seen also following the same bison. We were below, on a very steep hill-side, with the tigers above, and the bull between; only glimpses could be obtained of any of these animals—just the tips of the bison's horns would be seen now and then above the low jungle, and a passing shadowy view of a tiger. After going thus a long way, and the jungle getting denser, I left them, when, no doubt, the tigers dined on beef that night. I have seen where tigers had been eating a fresh-killed bison in a very thick bamboo cover at the bottom of a ravine we were crossing over. The smell and flies were horrible—great bits of meat, or limbs, rather, were strewed all round. This young cow had been most likely pounced upon, and pulled down by the united efforts of at least two tigers, or, perhaps, they had found a wounded one, shot by mistake, for the cows are never hunted, having inferior horns.

While wandering through these delightful jungles of Southern India in search of game, all sorts of curious animals will be seen and heard, also many strange birds, not to be met with in the other parts of India I have visited. An enormous butterfly, or "tussah"—silkmoth, rather—that was to be seen where "teak" trees in blossom were numerous, was especially astonishing, each wing being quite as large as the crown of a hat, or a common plate. On first meeting with them, flying about in the daytime under these tall, shady trees, I really thought they were some kind of owl, being of a brown colour; but afterwards frequently observed their peculiar flight, high up under the tallest teak trees, where a dozen or more together might be seen skimming around the scented teak blossoms, always in the shade.

Two sorts of monkeys were to be met with, one, the "Madras monkey," was to be seen, either in pairs or a family party of four or five, chiefly near cultivated spots, but also far away in the woods. These are the common little well-known brown monkey, so often seen tamed, and led about with organ grinders; but instead of the pale flesh-coloured face they all seem to have in confinement, these in the jungles had highly inflamed countenances—of a vermillion colour almost, that gave one the idea they had been visiting the "toddy trees" a little too often; but it may have been merely sun-burnt effects. The large "hunuman," or "langur" monkey, of a very light grey colour, and so common everywhere, was also to be seen in troops. These are the monkeys that are so useful to the sportsman, by giving notice, with a peculiar harsh coughing noise, of the presence of any tiger or panther prowling about—a very different call from the ordinary "hoop-hoop" noise they indulge in when not excited or alarmed. They were sometimes to be heard making a terrible noise, as if quarrelling most angrily among themselves, which was caused, according to native testimony, by the mothers having stolen, or playfully exchanged each other's babies; a grand chase after one another would generally be going on among the highest boughs, or tops of some immense, tall, wide-spreading forest trees.

While climbing a steep hill-side once, a monster "boa-constrictor" was observed moving along just above us. Its head was raised about six inches above the ground, but the rest of its length, quite five yards, or more, was straight, and glided onwards at a gentle walking pace (like a long "goods train" on a railway). On catching sight of us, it suddenly coiled itself up in rings, about two feet in diameter, and came rolling down the hill sideways, like a great curled, open shaving—so quickly, that we had to jump aside to avoid it in its course. It could easily have been shot, but was not fired at, for fear of disturbing the ground yet to be hunted over. At other times I have seen these big serpents asleep, and coiled up in caves, and have shot several, certainly six inches in diameter. They have the credit of being the monkey's worse enemy, climbing the tallest trees at night, and catching their prey asleep.

Once, a large "wolverine," or "waglee," as the natives term it, was stumbled on. It was quite a yard long, including the tail, and of a black colour—in shape like a gigantic ferret. It was busily engaged in eating a dead boar, that had been shot two days before for the men to eat while returning home, but could then nowhere be found. This brute has most powerful claws, and the natives have a story that it will drop on the back of a passing bison, and soon scratch such a hole in its skin that the liver can be got at and eaten—all this in spite of the bison's frantic efforts to rub off its enemy against trees and low branches. An improbable story, arising from the fact of this skunk being often found feeding on the carcase of any dead bison it may have come across, but mentioned here to show the sort of anecdote with which the hunter is occasionally regaled.

Ordinary snakes, of different sorts, were of course to be met with, daily almost; but here the cobras were nearly all of a light cane colour, instead of being black, as in other parts of India. While stalking on hands and knees, gazing intently ahead, where, perhaps, among the thick bushes only the bison's white stockings were to be seen a few yards off, I have been startled by seeing something move slightly quite close, which has turned out to be a long, straight, yellow snake, that no doubt was mistaken for a fallen bamboo when first glanced at. This gives one a nasty jerk.

The beautiful "jungle fowl" were very numerous everywhere. Their short, most shrill clear call of five sharp notes, was to be heard morning and evening on all sides. The cock is a splendid bird—so very like our tame barn-door cock, but larger and grander in every way, with even more brilliant plumage. The hens were of a uniform light reddish brown, mottled with darker brown and yellow specks, and without combs, of course. About a dozen hens seemed to accompany each fine old game-looking cock bird. Their eggs we often found—pale yellowish-white colour; but the chicks are said to be untameable. These birds would come trooping out of some shady bamboo-grown ravine, after it had been quietly beaten by a man or two tapping sticks or stones, while the hunter waited at the far end for whatever might appear, the men walking along the banks above and outside the cover—a beat only done on the return homewards after the day's work. I often cut over the cocks with a rifle ball; but they were always dreadfully tough to eat. The feathers are much prized by fishermen for making artificial flies.

The small "red spur fowl" were not nearly so numerous in

these jungles as in Central India or "Rajpootana." They are pretty little birds just the size of bantams, but of a dark red brown or chestnut colour. The cocks have two spurs on each leg, very marked and pointed, the hens mostly one spur on each leg and not so pronounced. They rustle along among the dead leaves and often make one believe something worth shooting is coming. They are also often to be heard calling, a sharp shrill note. These fowls too are uncommonly tough eating, but better if kept some little time. Both these jungle fowl are sometimes looked for by gunners in the hills with beaters and dogs; the dogs make them perch on low trees, when a snap shot can be had as they move off; they are extremely shy and wary fowls.

Formerly large herds of elephants used to frequent these forests, wandering up every year from the south, but they have discontinued the practice for some time. The men showed me where some years ago, on a herd having appeared and caused much mischief among a large gang of wood-cutters, employed by Government in felling the forest teak trees, killing some of the men I believe, a party of native police went in chase of the herd, and with their old "brown bess" muskets succeeded in killing some of the elephants, by liver shots no doubt. One female elephant on being wounded had twisted its trunk round a large branch, and so leaned or hung from it until dead; a "calf" was by her side. Never having had a chance of seeing elephants in a wild state, I can say nothing about them. On regretting this circumstance once before friends who had shot elephants, they told me for comfort perhaps that I had not lost much sport, for killing them with the enormous guns and charges now used was very like shooting a great pig. Still one does like to have a bang at every sort of wild animal for variety sake, not to mention the delight of watching every wild creature's habits in its native woods; however, they are not allowed to be hunted or shot now, very properly, being required for Government service.

All this gives but a very brief account of what the hunter may expect to meet with in bison shooting, for like hog hunting no two chases resemble one another. Brother sportsmen inform the novice of a thousand different adventures to be met with after this wary animal. I once wasted five successive days after a particular well-known old bull, and yet never got a shot at him. He lived in a very dense tangled mass of close-growing bamboo jungle near a village, with tolerably open ground all round, and never could be caught in the open, though I was often on the spot before daylight. His tracks could be traced into this patch of jungle, which was only about five hundred yards square; nor could he be driven out of it ever so early, for I often waited for him on the far side, but nothing ever appeared. Then would begin a hunt that lasted for several hours, but all in vain, for though silently creeping into the very spot where he had made a way for himself each morning at a different place, and with infinite trouble forcing a passage for myself through the same matted dense bamboo stumps (which had closed again after being pushed through by his great bulk and weight) and following through the tangled thorny undergrowth his wandering track in a most zigzag manner at the rate of about a hundred yards in half-an-hour, with the rifle at the "ready," getting hands, face, and neck scratched until not a quarter of an inch of skin could be found untorn, all at once—at one's very feet—up would jump this immense brute and crash through the cover at a racing pace, as if merely brushing through so much high grass or reeds. A tremendous crackling noise of smashed and splintered bamboos would be heard for a few seconds and then all would be still. Twice I got the merest glimpse of his exceedingly broad stern at only two yards distance, but it was of no use firing at that; besides, this rush would be so sudden and unexpected that there really was no time to take aim before the parted bamboos would close again, and then it was impossible to see one yard ahead, so dense was this matted jungle. He fairly beat me, so with much regret over so much lost time and labour I had to leave him alone.

The villagers were all afraid of this brute, especially at dawn when going to their fields. Nothing could make him leave this stronghold for another cover. Once when close upon him, two "minas," birds something like our starlings, suddenly made a most loud chattering noise from a low tree just overhead, when up jumped the bull, racing off with a snort and crash awful to listen to. He must have been asleep when these birds thus acted as sentinels, for reasons best known to themselves! Another step forward and I must have seen him and got a shot, most likely in a fair fatal place.

It is very provoking for the sportsman to find how the whole forest seems alive with different birds and animals that by calling or racing off seem bent on giving warning of his stealthy approach, as if all nature were in league against him. Monkeys will frequently "swear" or call after the hunter most persistently, mistaking perhaps his earth-brown clothes and creeping cautious movements for the tiger. Birds will fly out chattering loudly, evidently giving the alarm, which is passed on by others, till every head of game is wide awake and watching for the coming enemy.

Having a very good active bay pony, I have ridden right among a herd of bison. They were all cows feeding, and on hearing the clatter of the pony's unshod feet or hoofs climbing over some rocky broken ground, merely turned round their heads to gaze at us, but by stooping low down on the nag's neck I got within a dozen paces or so before being noticed, when there was a sudden squeal and general bolt of the whole herd down the hill, upon which until then they were quietly feeding, no doubt having scented self and pony.

Friends have told me of some very narrow escapes and accidents that have happened to themselves and men while after bison, so though this animal will try its best to escape from the hunter, still the exception to this rule is to be found, therefore caution is urged on the new hand at this kind of chase. The heavy arms used now-a-days of course lessen to almost nothing the chance of a mishap, always provided that they can be wielded effectually, and do not by their great weight tire or render the marksman unsteady at the critical moment. My pet weapon was a double breech-loading pin fire 12 bore "Henry" rifle, weight ten pounds, charge of powder 70 grains, or two and a half drams (it could not take more), with a conical bullet of nearly two ounces. With this I could be certain of hitting a cap box lid or shining mark of two inches diameter at seventy yards or more. The second rifle was an army short Snider with its Government ammunition. Great were my doubts often which of these two would be best to go armed with, when only one could be taken to the field. Both were quite up to any work required, which however did not include elephants, though the hardened tip of the Snider bullet would perhaps have been equal to even such an occasion. Being such light and handy weapons they could be brought to bear in a moment on any moving beast. Hares running were often rolled over for fun when all other work was done. For any kind of deer or long shooting the Snider was taken. Cost about three pounds.

This is merely mentioned so that the young hand should not be deterred from trying his luck as a hunter for want of an expensive "battery." Should the double gun be used with ball, remember that a light charge of three drams prevents many a miss at moving game, when only a snap shot can be taken, for then the gun is not jerked up high off the aim; besides the ball at starting will rise of itself from smooth bores, more especially so if overcharged—a common fault.

CHAPTER VIII.

LION SHOOTING.

DESCRIPTION OF LION—EFFECTS OF SHOTS—CATTLE PENS—FIVE SLEEPING BEAUTIES—AFFECTIONATE LIONESS—MANELESS LION—GALLANT LION—THE WILD ASS.

THE next description of "large game" is the "lion." These splendid animals are now only to be found in "Kattywar," Guzeerat, and a very few in Central India. They are precisely the same as the African lion, though formerly thought to be distinct, on account of having little or no mane. The first lion I shot in the "Gheer" Forest, Kattywar, had mane eighteen inches long and tolerably full, though not so shaggy and heavy as the African lions. This mane was of a uniform light brown colour, instead of being black as the latter are mostly described. He was a young male in his prime, certainly over ten feet six inches long, tail of course included, for on the skin being pegged down it measured eleven feet six inches, and was broad in proportion, without any signs of having been unduly stretched. Having nailed this skin against the wall of a room, on returning after a month's absence I found two large sparrow nests built of straw entwined in the long pendent hairs of the lion's mane, so firmly that they could not be removed without pulling out the hair also.

The occasion of finding this lion was on a friend and self being awakened one morning very early indeed, by a tremendous row going on, close to our small tent, of roaring and scuffling. At once guessing the cause, I slipped on a coat and shoes and hastened to the spot with a double rifle; there

Maj. Gen. W. Rice, Delt. Shaw & Sons, Lith.

LION SHOOTING.

a cattle herdsman was driving off his buffaloes in great haste, using the long stout stick covered with iron rings they all carry for the purpose. One tame buffalo was lying dead on the ground, which was a clear open space, with but few small trees scattered about. The man pointed to a large thick "corindah" bush close by, and hastened after his cattle. I walked on tip-toe to this bush with the rifle quite ready, but when within a dozen yards a low growl was heard; nothing whatever could be seen through the dense foliage, so silently stepping back, I went round in a circle and tried to get a view from the opposite sides, but on again getting close more growling was heard, but nothing could be made out, even indistinctly, so again walking away backwards, it occurred to me to wait over the fresh killed buffalo's body. There was a small "bastard teak" tree close by, so I quietly stepped up its low sloping trunk, and there waited quite concealed by the thick leaves, some small branches of which I silently bent down, half broken, to make the cover closer all round. It was only about four feet from the ground, but there really was no other hiding place near. After waiting a few minutes only, the lion crawled very slowly out of the bush and began walking towards the buffalo, step by step, and looking carefully round on all sides; his bright white fangs were plainly visible as he came slowly on. At about twenty-five paces off he turned slightly sideways, when I sent a "shell" into his flank, which shot I distinctly heard burst inside him. Instantly with a teriffic roar he bounded forward full stretch, and clearing quite thirty yards in three long bounds, rolled over under a small bush, when a choking "guggle-guggle" noise in his throat, very pleasant to hear, told me it was all right. On skinning this lion we found particles of the shell, like flattened shots in his body.

Over night I had sat up in a low tree, directly over a path leading to the village (near which our tent was pitched(, having heard that this lion was in the habit of constantly prowling around the place and roaring at night. There was a very bright moon, but on getting down from the tree, after a two hours' wait, until the moon went down, I found by marks previously made in the sand that the lion had passed and repassed immediately under the low tree, not two yards off from where I was waiting above, but owing to the lion's colour being so exactly the same as the ground around, it was not seen, although the full moonlight was clear enough to read by. Long lines drawn in the sand across the path before getting into the tree, proved this fact, for his prints both coming and going were plainly to be seen over the marks which were made to see if he visited the village at all that night, so as to be able next morning to follow him up. This was the largest lion shot out of fourteen killed in ten days' hunting. They stand about three feet six inches high, but the lioness is smaller in every way and more slimly built. Their footprints were very round compared with a tiger's, and quite six inches in diameter as shown on the sandy ground.

These lions were of various shades of light brown, mostly the same colour as a camel, from which cause they are often called by natives, the "camel tiger," or "unteea wagh." The name for the male in these parts was "sawuj," the lioness was called "sooee," but "sheer" for both is the usual name elsewhere. One young lion killed was of a bright brown sugar colour, with a hog mane just springing up. When killed they all had a fine noble expression, almost benevolent, having nothing of the vicious look about the face of panthers or tigers; and a curious fact was that one bullet apiece sufficed to kill each animal, very different from a tiger who is often very lively with a dozen bullets in him. One lion on being shot in the neck, spun round and round like a wounded dog. The shock of a bullet seemed to have very great effect on a lion's frame, perhaps from a slight mixture of dog, in their otherwise true cat nature.

These animals besides preying on all kinds of deer, hog, nil-ghai, the wild ass on the desert border, samber, &c., kill cattle and buffaloes in great numbers. On this account the cattle owners build high stockades of stout young trees placed side by side and firmly fastened together with cross beams. Into these places of refuge the cattle are all driven every night at sunset, and there remain huddled up together until next dawn. These large pens, called "neiss," are about twenty yards square, with the tree stumps about fifteen feet high, pointed at the top, and are built outside most villages. Here on night coming on the lions meet in twos and threes and walk round and round, sniffing and scratching at the stout palings, like terrier dogs at a rat hole, giving an occasional roar that greatly terrifies the closely packed cattle within. Towards dawn the lions walk off into the dense forest, roaring at intervals as they go.

From this custom of theirs, it was easy by listening attentively to guess in which direction to hunt for them, when the day had got hot and they were asleep in their several lairs, either dry sandy caves or very thick shady bushes, hollowed out underneath like bowers with wide overhanging branches. Here they could be followed up by their fresh footprints, all these places of resort and sleeping being well known to the villagers.

On one occasion with the trackers we came up to a thick "corindah" bush, just outside of which was a fresh killed "cheetal" deer lying, having been dragged there; while inside the bush five full-grown lions were to be seen, all fast asleep and lying side by side, heads and tails foremost like so many pigs in a sty. This was rather too much to be pleasant! so silently stepping back on the soft sandy ground, a consultation in whispers was held, which ended in our party being spread round the bush, each gun at about fifty yards distance, when a sudden loud shouting from all sides started out the five lions, each running off half awake and much confused in a different direction. They were all shot there and then, without any following up being required. One hunter, Dr. E. B., was lucky enough to kill two lions, with a right and left shot, a feat not often to be recorded! Following up a wounded lion is considered most awkward work, for they have the credit of making their charge home good, and of not swerving on one side when fired at close enough to singe them almost, as I have known to be the case with tigers on more than one occasion; but of this fact or firm behaviour on the lion's part I cannot speak, having luckily found all wounded ones dead, after following up.

Once I very nearly stepped on a sleeping lioness while passing over the large outspreading root of a fallen decayed tree. She jumped up and raced off among the high dry grass all around. Thinking it was only a deer, and wishing to get some meat for the pot, I ran after her, hoping to get a distant shot. After going about two hundred paces the lioness stopped short and looked round at me, when for the first time I saw it was a lion, being then about thirty yards off. Pulling up with a jerk I stooped slowly down in the high grass; the lioness kept looking first at me, and then on one side, and then again at me, for about five minutes. It was useless trying for a shot at her head, she so constantly moved it, so I chose a shot behind the shoulder, keeping the left barrel with a "shell" in it in reserve. Off bounded the lion, while I knelt down quite low on firing, to be out of sight. Evening setting in, prevented our following it up far enough, as it became too dark to find the dead game; but on resuming the search next day at dawn, the lioness was found very little beyond where overnight's blood and prints had been taken, but the skin was completely spoilt, for the jackals had eaten it away on one flank. These curs never touch a dead tiger or panther either, no doubt mistrusting them as shamming sleep.

Having on one occasion skinned a lion in the jungle and carried the skin home to the small tent, about midnight a lioness was heard quite close moaning all night long in a most sorrowful manner; this noise was at times changed for a low angry roar. Sleeping on the ground at the time and not being more than thirty paces or less distant, the sound appeared to come in successive waves or rolling vibrations from her mouth held low down to the ground. The horses were particularly alarmed; more wood was piled on the four large fires, one on each side, a precaution always taken before turning in for the night, and several shots were fired in the air, but she still remained moaning and roaring. The night being very dark nothing was to be seen, and the beast was thought to be lying in a small ravine close by. Just at daybreak she went off back to the forest roaring at every five minutes' space as their custom is. Directly it was light enough this lioness was followed up by its prints, and then we found she had taken, in coming to the tent, the very path by which the skin had been brought home over night, and could see where at times she had stopped where drops of blood had fallen by the way. Most affecting, some near relative no doubt ! but this did not save her own skin, for she was soon found and shot. At first the people would give no assistance whatever to help find these lions, but when they saw we could manage without their help they volunteered freely enough, being glad to be rid of such enemies.

Once afterwards when passing a village near which we had hunted the previous year, the people begged me earnestly to wait while their young men ran off to mark down any sleeping lions. It seems that after killing several cattle belonging to this place, an old lion would every evening come out of the forest and lie down, stretched out on a large piece of flat stone or sheet rock close to the village; presently he would look round, when a lioness used to follow and lie down by his side; she again was followed by another young half-grown lion, and there the three would wait. At last one of the men, with the rest of the populace behind him, took a steady kneeling shot with a matchlock at the old lion, but somehow missed or merely grazed him, for the lion thereupon bounded forward, and after nearly pulling the marksman's head off, retreated to the woods with his mate and cub. To my sorrow I could not wait to settle matters with this old lion, having been called on most urgent business to a neighbouring town.

Formerly lions were far more plentiful in this part of the country, and used to live more in the open plains. One cavalry officer a good many years ago, told me he had shot eighty lions in this province in three years, using well-trained horses for the purpose, and following them over the open country. His gun was a small bore double-barrel flint one, for he described the horror on rushing to a friend's rescue, who had been seized by the arm by a wounded lioness, of finding that after snapping several times in vain, the gun flint had fallen out and a new one had to be screwed in, when the lioness was killed by a shot fired close into its ear.

From being so constantly hunted, lions have left the open plains almost, and betaken themselves chiefly to the forests, where the numerous thorn bushes must drag out the best part of their manes, until they cease by degrees to have any left, except the very old lions. This is supposed to be the reason of the "maneless lion of Guzeerat" being considered a distinct species, a title imperfectly accorded.

Lions wander considerably, travelling all night and lying up in the day time, at certain to them well-known resting places. They often go in company as many as six or more at times, and seem to keep to the same rounds in travelling. From this cause the above named friend, the noted lion hunter, Colonel D., told me his "shikarree" used to watch over a few well-known regular halting places of the lions, and bring him news of a fresh arrival, when he would ride out to the spot, shoot the lion, and again in a few days another lion would be reported as having taken up its quarters in the self-same bush or den, when it also would be killed. Once he described how his hunter, while they were following up the fresh prints of a lion, knelt down to look under a thick bush. After a very long silent pause the man withdrew his head from the bush, when his countenance was observed to be "green." The poor fellow had all this time been staring at a lion asleep, face to face at almost kissing distance; having been stricken dumb and dazed he could merely make a few signs by pointing to the bush, when the lion was shot asleep.

This gentleman also killed a large "black lion," very old, and for many years known to frequent the country round "Goondul," Kattywar. This name was given the beast, on account of its dark mane, and dusky hide generally. When travelling and wandering over the country in this manner, lions will put up for the day, under any kind of shelter, for I have known two turned out from under a haystack, even—while cane fields afford a temporary refuge. Their usual course is through large patches of dry grass, extending often for many miles, and preserved for feeding cattle. These extensive tracts help to hide the lions in their journeys from one set of hills or jungles to some far distant range, or fresh hunting grounds.

The best place to fire at seems to be just behind the shoulder, half-way up, but not too close to the shoulder-blades. This will be the liver shot again; and they do not go far when so hit, while little or no blood is to be seen, for they bleed to death internally; and "following up" a short time afterwards is safe work enough. The small prickle at the very end of the tail, embedded among the hairs, easily comes off on being touched. It is barely half an inch long, and looks like dried skin almost, but was formerly supposed to be used for lashing the lion into a proper state of rage by self-spurring.

A native officer, Jemedar J. K., of the Joonaghur State, has shot an immense number of lions in the vast "Gheer Forest," their chief abode. He computed that there were not above three hundred lions left altogether in that country. One of his men—a splendid hand at everything connected with lion shooting arrangements and tracking—described how once waiting for deer, up a large, wide-spreading tree, with his loaded matchlock, a pair of lions appeared on the scene—evidently a courtship was being carried on. Presently the lioness, on coming just under the tree, was shot dead seemingly. At once the male lion, in a most furious rage, commenced a series of wild charges at nothing on all sides, with terrific roars, always returning to and fondling the prostrate lioness. At last he took her up by the back of the neck, and walked off with the lioness thrown over his shoulder. The hunter, being joined by some companions, started in pursuit, but, though these men followed the very plain marks of this pair of lions for a long way, neither of them was ever seen again. This lioness, having been merely stunned, must have recovered and gone off with her lover, after being so affectionately carried by him far out of further danger.

Having to leave this part of India, no further chance was offered me of again hunting lions; but I feel certain a rare bag of them could be made by any one getting the requisite leave of absence for the purpose. The chief drawback to hunting in this particular forest, called the "Gheer," is its extreme unhealthiness, owing to the very bad water obtainable; also the great heat, something unbearable by new comers to the country. The water, before being drunk, had to be invariably boiled. Formerly, this jungle forest must have been very populous, for the ruins of decayed towns and villages were to be seen every few miles apart. The lions will be found chiefly on the outskirts of this vast jungle, which greatly lessens the risk of getting fever from living long in these woods; for the sportsman's tent can be pitched out in the plains around, where it is healthy enough. The lions, no doubt, find it easier to live on the village cattle found grazing on the borders of the forest to hunting up samber, cheetal, &c., in the steep hills with which the country is covered, especially in the midst of the "Gheer."

Referring to the "wild ass," mentioned above, these animals will be found in herds of two or three hundred together sometimes, also in batches of six or seven, feeding on the rank grass to be seen among the sand-hills on the borders of the "Runn" of Cutch, a vast sandy desert plain, also on the desert borders of Scinde. They are very shy and difficult to approach—at the same time so fleet that it is hopeless to get near them, unless one has been first wounded by a long shot. These asses wheel round in formation just like so many cavalry. The native name is "khur guddrey," signifying desert donkey. They are about twelve hands high at the shoulder, and of a sandy pinkish colour. Nobody thinks of molesting them, except for curiosity sake. The foals are sometimes ridden down when very young, and caught—for they can be tamed easily, as pets, but not for working purposes. One used to run loose about Camp Ahmedabad—a general favourite.

CHAPTER IX.

TIGER SHOOTING.

THE GHAUT, OR HILL TIGER—LENGTH OF TIGERS—OVER OLD SHOOTING GROUND—METHOD OF HUNTING—FATAL SHOTS—TRACKING—FOLLOWING UP.

Now comes the "tiger." This grand beast, whose very name never fails to rouse attention—India's own and best of sport. There is no need to waste time in describing such a well-known animal, except, perhaps, to here remark, that on the Ghauts of Western India, opposite Goa, I have seen and examined a fresh-killed tiger, evidently full-grown and very old, whose appearance was so totally different from any ordinary tiger, that, except for its stripes, I should have felt sure it must have been some distinct species. Its length, including tail, which was comparatively short, was about eight feet only. The head was of a most round and bull-dog shape. The fore arms very short, but most massive, chest not at all deep, but very wide, while the body, towards the hind quarters, fell off greatly, and the stomach was tucked up almost like a greyhound's—the hind legs being particularly small and slight, like a panther's. The brute looked all fore arms and shoulders, with the little round bull-dog head before mentioned. The stripes were very few, and but faintly marked, and the ground colour a dirty yellow, where pure white would have been on a common tiger. It could not have stood over two feet high. No doubt this extraordinary variation in form and appearance of this particular breed of tiger has been caused by a continued course, through ages past, of climbing and hunting over the precipitous mountain range of these districts. It looked like a dwarf tiger. This was the only specimen met with ; but I have heard of others being seen like it on these ghauts. Several other tigers killed and seen in this part of Southern India, had nothing peculiar in their appearance.

The book called "Tiger Shooting in India," referred to sport obtained in Rajpootana districts while stationed at Camp Nemuch, with my late regiment, the 25th Bombay Native Light Infantry, during some leave, extending over four hot seasons—from 1850. Before, and in those days, tigers were almost invariably looked for and shot at from a secure sort of box, called a "howdah," strapped on the backs of elephants, with what would now be considered very light, inferior weapons for the purpose, being chiefly smooth bore double muzzle loading guns, of about "No. 17 bore," carrying an ounce spherical ball, with a charge of about 2½ drams of powder. Rifles, except single ones, with a block or "standing sight," for nothing under one hundred yards, were very little known, and seldom used, not being then thought handy or quick enough for such snap-shooting, though, perhaps, useful for a distant retreating shot, always provided that the elephant could be coaxed to stand still enough at the time of firing—a rare event indeed.

Not being able to afford the cost of elephants, and finding the country, from its hilly nature, would admit in almost all cases of hunting tigers on foot, the author then made the attempt, and with tolerable success. Since those times—thanks to the wonderful improvements in firearms—shooting every sort of big game on foot has become quite the fashion, so it is hoped these pages may help to show the young sportsman how elephants may be dispensed with in many places.

Starting, at first, alone on these hunting expeditions, and afterwards being joined at intervals by one or more friends, the "bag" made during these trips consisted of sixty-eight tigers killed, and thirty tigers wounded; seven panthers killed and wounded; and fifty-one bears killed and wounded—grand total, one hundred and fifty-six head of large game killed and wounded. Besides these, several other beasts are confidently believed to have been wounded, but are not included in the list, as no blood could be found to clearly prove the fact. This was the invariable test, but not always a correct one.

N.B.—All the measurements recorded of tigers, &c., were taken after the skins had been pegged down, being well stretched in so doing; but great pains were taken to insure these skins presenting their proper relative breadth as well as length; and it will be found that when thus fairly pegged out, not much can be added to a skin; but as some doubt has been expressed as to the extraordinary length of many of the tigers mentioned in the aforesaid book, it may be as well to state that several animals seemingly far larger than any killed were seen at close distances, and escaped wounded or otherwise.

The average size of tigers in that part of Rajpootana where, until then, they had hardly ever been disturbed, was certainly far larger than any seen by my men or self in other parts of India. An extract from the *Bombay Gazette* newspaper of 19th July, 1873, is as follows: "Length "of Tigers.—Colonel Beresford writes to a contemporary, 'I "'have measured many tigers, and though I should say that, "'on an average, 10 feet 6 inches for a male, and 9 feet 8 "'inches for a female, is about the mark, I do not agree "'with those who say that anything over 11 feet is a stretch "'of imagination, if not of cuticle. I myself shot a tiger in "'1862, whom I measured as he lay on the ground as 12 feet

"'4 inches; that skin was NEVER stretched; the carcase was "'brought to cantonments, and skinned by the man who "'cured it. As I say, it then measured 12 feet 4 inches, and "'that skin in England at this moment measures 11 feet "'6 inches. I also remember two other tigers, whom I "'measured as they lay, of the respective lengths of 11 feet "'2 inches, and 11 feet 4 inches.'" On my subsequently mentioning this subject to some famous Bheel hunters, they at once remarked, "Why not?—Are all men the same size?"

The part of the country near Camp Neemuch in Rajpootana, where "big game" are to be found, consisted of long ridges of low hills, of a broken, rocky nature; also the more steep hill-sides of long, higher ranges, flat on the top, and for the most part bare, except for a few scattered jungle trees, or where the plateau was covered with the high, coarse, turpentine grass, called "jaum." Along these hill ranges, at close distances, would be seen deep rocky ravines, in many of which flowing water was to be met with, from springs above. These ravines, or "korees," as they are called, would be covered with dense jungle of various sorts, such as bamboo clumps, "corinda" bushes, thorn bushes of many kinds, while large mango trees, date, and "mowra" trees, besides tamarind, "peepul," and nearly all the common jungle timber of sorts would be found at the base, forming almost groves, of great length. The spaces between these ravines were comparatively bare and open; but with immense boulders of rock, rolled down from above, scattered over their sides and below. All these shady places afforded excellent cover for game of every sort to lie up in, being beautifully sheltered and cool.

At the foot of these hill ranges were many rivulets, more or less dry, in places running far out into the plains beyond. The beds of these streams would be covered for lengths at intervals with dense matted low jungle, mixed up with and growing out of large rocks, jumbled together in endless confusion, while their banks on both sides would be shaded for long stretches with the beautiful light green willow tree called "jummonea" and patches of another sweet-smelling kind of willow bush called "neegrah," all these shady places, but especially the last named, forming the very best and likeliest possible cover for tigers to lie up in, also bears, panthers, hog, and deer innumerable. The ground near the rivers would be sandy, so very easy to take tracks up on or see what had gone into any particular patch of cover, water in long sheets dividing these strips of jungle at every few hundred yards or so. No better country for hunting over could possibly be imagined, for if an animal was not at home in one patch of jungle, the chances were he would be started out of the next.

Villages at about every three miles were to be seen, but very small ones, a dozen huts forming the average, while far out in the open plains, both above and below these ranges of hills, would be found other immense ravines, often of great depth and breadth, with water flowing through their length, their sides and bottoms being covered with dense bamboo and every sort of shady jungle. These ravines gave one the idea of having been formed by some mighty convulsion of nature, such as earthquakes. They were frequently stumbled upon most unexpectedly, the surrounding country seeming quite plain and level, when on approaching within a few yards of their sides deep chasms and in places perfect precipices would be come upon most suddenly.

Nothing could be more beautiful and cheering than this change from the hot, bare, rocky ground around to looking down on these cool, shady green covers, more especially as you felt perfectly certain that they would hold some sort of big game. Never was such a paradise for the hunter, but they have been greatly worked and thinned since those days, the whole country then being like an undiscovered land, for on the best district maps was written for miles round "No information forthcoming of this part" at the time of my first visit. The natives seemed quite unacquainted with English sportsmen and their rifles, for the country was not considered quite safe to wander over, while the people seemed to fear giving any assistance, lest they should incur the displeasure of the numerous petty chiefs around; but a better race than these "Meenas" and jungle inhabitants generally for shikar matters could not be wished for, while the aforesaid chiefs and people of the larger towns were as objectionable as they usually are, being naturally opposed to the presence of the infidel European. Moreover, just then the Mutiny was ripening apace. The usual plan was to collect from the neighbouring villages as many men as were willing to come, twenty being considered quite enough, and then drive one of these likely ravines, the sportsman being posted either at the end of it or just over some particular opening where game was known to be in the habit of breaking cover. These spots were called "naka" or "moule," meaning outlets or bolting points, and had to be carefully selected and well looked at before deciding to keep guard over them, for it often happened that they had been so considered merely from custom, some chief and his followers having perhaps ages ago seen fit to think them suited for the purpose, while a little beyond or short of the suggested place would be discovered perfect points of advantage, taking in every possible loophole for escape.

It was some time before the necessity of being thus cautious in choosing every place of ambuscade over the covers generally was forced upon me from animals creeping off safe and undiscovered in the most disgusting manner, when all too late the obviously ill-chosen point over which guard had been kept would be too plainly apparent. This mistake was mostly found out on taking up the prints of the escaped quarry directly afterwards with bitter feelings of disappointment.

Having once discovered this famous ground, it soon became evident that the best plan was to keep to it, instead of wasting much time and labour as at first befell me, being a perfect stranger to this part of the country and peculiar dialect even, in looking for fresh hunting fields farther off, for not only did the ground become more bare and open, with less chance of holding game, but the people were still less inclined to assist the greater distance one wandered from Camp Neemuch. So each hot weather hunting trip was passed in visiting the same covers two or three times in succession, a regular circuit being laid out for the purpose. By this means one became not only well acquainted with all the villagers likely to act as beaters, who in their turn were most willing to give every information, but also the likeliest places to look up the big game. These people soon seeing how easily the tigers were killed were very glad to help, for their cattle used to suffer tremendously. A tiger would quarter himself on a village and regularly kill his cow or bullock every third day. A frightful tax!

The whole of this happy hunting ground was comprised in a district about seventy miles long by thirty miles wide, a very pretty preserve in a ring fence as it were, for the big game never ventured to cross the surrounding wide cultivated level plains, but stuck to their fastnesses in the steep, broken, hilly waste jungles aforesaid. This is how the beat or drive was generally managed. Having collected the required number of men, and the likeliest cover or where the latest "kill" of cattle, deer, &c., was known to have occurred being selected, the hunter would start off for his post with two men carrying the spare guns and water bag or "chagul." On arriving at the spot where he was to wait in ambush, these two men would be sent back silently to join the rest of the beaters and tell them that all was ready to begin. If the cover was a very long one, with several side branches or smaller ravines leading into it by which animals would be likely to break sideways, these places had to be carefully guarded by placing single men up trees to turn them back as already described in the process of ringing a bear, &c. The best plan for this most needful precaution was to go with each man yourself and see him quietly and properly posted alone up the tree. Once left there it was not likely that he would attempt to quit the spot, knowing that the noise of the beaters would very shortly turn out a tiger or two, which he would have to run the risk of meeting on foot. It never answered to place two men together for this work; they would be certain to begin talking and so spoil the whole affair by driving back the game started on to the beaters, or causing it to break away at some other open part of the cover. Of course, if the game was moving properly on to the front, these men up trees remained perfectly silent and motionless, having then nothing to do but keep an eye on it and watch the course taken by the beast should it attempt to return or go in any other wrong direction, so as to be able to warn the beaters on their passing his post or tree.

To enable the men beating these covers to make as much noise as possible they were provided with four kettle-drums, called "tansees," made of tin, with a goat's skin tightly braced over the top. These instruments, struck with a short, slight cane, emitted a most discordant noise. A big bell was also provided, which made as much row as any dinner bell. This was intended to imitate the bells often worn round the neck by elephants belonging to the native chiefs who occasionally got up hunting parties among these jungles. There was also a big drum made of tin, with two goats' skins stretched over either end. This was very light and portable, and always to be heard above the rest. My own Shikarrees (a Bheel and a Mharatta) were entrusted with a pair of old horse pistols and a horn each filled with coarse gunpowder, with which they fired blank shots at invervals. These repeated discharges greatly encouraged the beaters, for they knew no large game would wait for them to almost step upon when it heard such frequent shots coming onwards.

There were also two old army halberts, formidable looking spears, which served to keep the body of men well together in passing through high grass or the thick green reeds called "banzeel," often high overhead, for all could see their broad, sharp, glittering points. The villagers had their own drawn swords, bows and arrows, and short spears, while every one carried his hatchet as usual in his waist-cloth, and many wore slings round their heads according to custom, or carried them ready, for all started with a good supply of stones in their waist-bags. These too could be picked up during the advance. Stones were slung or thrown with wonderful force and aim into every likely looking bush, and were most useful for starting any tiger that might be disposed to lurk too long in cover or refuse to move at all as sometimes happened. These last would be some cunning old beasts that had been driven before and shot at by the aforesaid native chiefs, or who guessed the trap laid for their destruction. All the men were directed to always keep in as compact a body as possible, no straggling, and to make their utmost yelling and noise, which they certainly did with a will.

This procession, which always moved very slowly and carefully, was called the "band." There was not the slightest danger to any one taking part in such a movement, for the din was so great that no animal liked waiting for it;

and by all keeping thus well together the cover would be driven far better than if the men had been spread out in a dangerously thin line, as if merely looking for hares or such small game. A tiger or any big animal wounded or otherwise would be very apt to rush back past a line of single beaters, knocking over one or more perhaps in so doing, whereas in this close formation, if these animals ever did bolt back, there was always plenty of space for them to get by on either side.

From time to time, as the body of beaters moved onwards, one of their number would nimbly climb any tree in passing, and so by keeping a good look-out on all sides be able to view any big game that was moved. If the fresh prints of a just disturbed tiger were seen, or the place where one had been lying down observed, or the beast itself viewed, the two blank pistol shots were fired quickly together. These double shots acted as notice of what was to be expected to the hunter in ambush ahead, and were very pleasant to hear. They moreover prevented him thinking of firing at any less noble game than a tiger. On hearing these signal shots several times bears have been allowed to pass on free, even three or four together, that otherwise must have been easily killed. A panther was the exception to this strict rule, chiefly on account of its beautiful skin, and because these brutes were considered by the natives quite as dangerous to their cattle as the tiger itself.

Up to this time the body of beaters have been sitting down at one end of the cover, smoking of course and talking as usual, waiting the return of the men who went with the spare guns, &c., to post the sportsman, or else the time they were told to allow for any such preparations before commencing the beat has elapsed. Now all being in readiness the "band" strikes up a most insufferable din, while some single blank pistol shots are at once fired for safety sake.

The moment this awful row commences it is most curious to note the sudden change from the perfect stillness that reigns in the jungles during the great mid-day heat. Clouds of startled green parrots, wood pigeons also green (of which, by-the-bye, there are three sorts, all very good eating), doves in swarms, a large horned owl or two, and pea fowl in numbers come sweeping by in the greatest alarm. Monkeys, the large grey "hoonuman," for there are none other in Rajpootana, begin to loudly call their "hoop," "hoop" noise, to be soon changed for their other note of alarm, the loud, husky, repeated cough or swearing as it sounds like, should either tiger or panther be afoot. In all these cool shady ravines peacocks are found in great numbers, and very useful indeed they are, for from their cry the hunter can tell to a certainty almost if a tiger or panther is moving about the cover. At the first alarm of the band these birds begin calling to one another, a sort of warning note "hank," "h-a-n-k," as from a trumpet; but if this is changed to their loud "tok-tok," "tok-tok," cry, uttered evidently in the wildest state of alarm as each bird rises in succession and flies off still screaming or calling, it may be set down as certainly having been caused by their being flushed at the sight of a tiger or panther moving out and coming upon them most unexpectedly. Nothing can be finer than to watch these grand peacocks viewed from above on the steep sides of a deep ravine. As they skim along in their flight, the sun shining on their long tails, they seem to leave a lengthened, quivering wave of light in their wake, for scores will be seen gliding past, a truly splendid sight.

Presently the distant din becomes still more audible, the "band" has turned a corner of the ravine, and now is heard the double shots from the horse pistols, followed by extra shouts and yells of the men, with perhaps the loud sudden "wough" of a tiger, who has been startled by the dreadful row from some shady retreat that he had intended to lie up hid in, letting the beaters pass, but now finds he must break forward. This in the middle of the hot weather is no joke, for the burning sand and stones, with in places rocks, that will blister the feet if stood on for half a minute even, have to be passed over, not to mention the annoyance of having been awakened from sleep, so the beast is naturally in a most vicious state of rage and fright combined. However, on he comes at a steady trot, hoping to get clear off and away to some other distant hiding place, and if previously not fired at, keeping no very sharp look-out, which must be rather difficult to do in the blinking glare of broad daylight and heat dancing in the air, as appears to be the case on these broiling days. But should the tiger happen to be one that has had to run the gauntlet on some former occasion, then his pace will be stealthy and cautious in the extreme, peering well ahead and around at every step, stopping to listen again and again, with short halts at large bushes and under each immense boulder, rock, &c.

It now behoves the sportsman to keep as quiet and still as possible, not moving a finger even, and if the rifle has to be cocked it must be done noiselessly and without any jerking or moving of the gun barrels (as many clumsy gunners often do), for the tiger's hearing and vision on these occasions are both most acute; the glimmer of the gun moving being especially liable to attract his attention. Of course the hunter will have taken care to have his dress of an uniform brown colour, without any white or conspicuous shining objects about him, his hat too being of the same brown or dark green colour, while all signs of white collars or shirts are quite invisible.

All these precautions are indispensable, or the animal instead of coming properly on and so affording a steady killing shot, will bound back with a roar very likely, and at a pace that makes hitting very doubtful indeed, or else by slowly dropping down in the low grass cover, he will silently and gradually back himself out of sight in denser cover around, in both cases making it dangerous in the extreme for the beaters, for in this race back he would charge any unfortunate straggler met in his way, separated ever so little from the other men in a compact body; or else by hiding close and lying perfectly flat, the unsuspecting beaters thinking the cover either a blank draw or that the game must have sneaked off unperceived ahead or broken away sideways, will very probably almost step on this crouching brute, when up it jumps most unexpectedly with terrible roars, and is pretty sure to bolt back past the crowd of men now thrown into the utmost confusion.

These are the occasions when sad accidents happen, the tiger bent on making good its escape, striking out wildly at all opposing scattered persons found in its way. But say that it is coming on properly, either at the unsuspicious jog-trot pace, or crawling inch by inch at the most stealthy rate, in either case the hunter must wait before firing until the beast has cleared or is certainly more than opposite his post, when the shot can be given safely enough, for the tiger is then certain to bound forward in its efforts to get clear past his hidden enemy. This allows the band and beaters to continue their onward movement.

On hearing the hunters' shots and the loud "wough," "wough!" that is sure to be pumped out of the tiger on his being fired at, for hit or not in his rage this angry grunt is pretty sure to be uttered, the men should be instructed to redouble if possible their previous din, which they luckily are almost sure to do of their own accord, for this extra noise will prevent a confused wounded tiger having any idea of trying to bolt back again, as well as perhaps helping to start forward a second beast or more should they be in the same cover. Nothing helps to give the men confidence in the hunter more than this act of consideration for their safety, viz., the knowledge that no animal will ever be fired at between themselves and the gunner. It is a very stupid mistake to do so under any circumstances, but some raw hands get so excited at the first glimpse of the game, that "bang," "bang," goes the gun, without any thought of waiting for a far better and safer shot. For these reasons the hunter should never be posted at the extreme end of a cover, but always leave a little bit over, which can be guarded from his ambush, to still admit of the wounded game rushing forward; so again the tiger on reaching the very end of any strip of jungle is sure to take a very careful prolonged stare ahead before breaking away across the open, and then is very apt to discover in time for retreat his would-be murderer.

Now as to where to fire at the passing or already passed tiger—if it is a slow-creeping cautious brute within reasonable distance, say twenty to thirty yards, a good rifle shot will kill it dead by a ball through the head or ear, and so save further trouble; but it should be borne in mind that the tiger's brain is comparatively a very small one, and lies in a long narrow cell at the extreme top of the skull, so can be easily missed. Under the fore arm, half way up the breadth of the body is not bad, for this goes through the lungs and soon disables the brute; care must be taken however not to hit the shoulder, which is so thick and muscular as to be almost certain to turn aside the bullet, causing it to glance under the skin in any direction, but decidedly the best shot and easiest is to fire at what will break the liver; this is a large mark quite eight inches round—aim about six inches, or one-third of the animal's depth of body from the top of its back, and just about half of its entire length, a good centre shot in fact. Don't shoot too low down in the flank or only the paunch will be struck, a most useless shot perfectly harmless at the time, and one that will not kill the game till several days afterwards. Try hard to remember exactly where the bullet struck, for on the men coming up there will be much questioning on this point, and a concise answer is expected. Of course the second barrel is fired as well, if possible, and as many others that can be poured in with certainty, but there is seldom much chance of getting more than two good clear shots, for one mighty bound mostly lands the tiger out of sight in the thick jungle ahead.

The certainty of having scored a good centre shot in the liver makes the coming "following up" process a far more pleasant one than any other hit, for the tiger will be invariably found dead after going about 150 yards or so choked from internal bleeding. By listening attentively after such a good shot, often the sounds of coughing will be heard, followed by crashing of bushes, when all is still, these last sounds being caused by the animal's death flurry. A liver shot will often leave no signs of blood anywhere, except on finding the defunct brute bleeding from the nose, but marks of the tiger's claws stretched wide out at each bound for about thirty yards will show plainly enough that a fatal wound has been given. At other times, whether hit or not, the marks of these open claws on the ground will not be seen beyond two bounds at most, if at all, being then caused by rage and fright only combined, for alighting so on the open foot with outspread claws is most unnatural and must jar the animal. Except for killing purposes the claws are at all times kept carefully sheathed, though there is the exception to this rule when tigers take to scratching the soft bark of trees, often six or eight feet high up the trunk. These long-scored marks are frequently met with in the woods and are not to be mistaken, though bears also will mark the trees in this manner, but not so high up, and their handiwork is different.

Tigers again will often scratch at tufts of high coarse dry

grass, as if for cleaning their nails; they also scratch as a dog does with their hind feet, leaving two long wide marks, called "kencheela," mostly by the side of any path or road. These signs are always to be well observed, for by their freshness the tiger is known to be in the neighbourhood. The fresh marks of his feet are of course the chief certain signs to work upon; these on being discovered are noticed most carefully, spots of dew will help to tell they were made during the night, the wind too helps to point out their freshness or otherwise by blowing down or away the fine edges inside the toe prints and around the footmark generally. Expert trackers will be able to tell within a very short time when the trail was made. A male's print can be distinguished from the tigress or young tiger's footmark almost to a certainty, the first named being often five inches wide.

These newly-found tracks are covered with a small bough or thorn bush placed over them in any path, to prevent cattle or people passing that way obliterating them until it is decided whether they shall be carried on or not. A ring at the same time is drawn completely round the footmark as a sign of its having been observed by the hunters, while in tracking or carrying on the prints, a short line is drawn in the dust just before each toemark. This is most useful, for if the trail is ever lost while following it the trackers step back to the last made scratch, and from that point try to recover it by taking extra pains to again hit upon the proper course. All take care to stand wide on one side of any trail in following it, and avoid pressing on the trackers or hurrying them in the least, for at a fault of course the rate is very slow indeed, but when hit off again, it can often be carried on at a walking pace.

Marks or indications of where the animal has been are often so very faint as to be invisible to inexperienced eyes, even when pointed out, but these men of the woods from constant practice decipher them with ease. Great attention and interest in the subject will soon help the sportsman to attain some little skill in this most useful and necessary part of all hunting business, while the smallest proficiency in the science helps to give him confidence and a feeling of independence as well. The far too flattering remarks of the Shikarrees, "he can 'pug'" (that is, track animals), at the same time pointing to the author, was always received with a stare of astonishment and grin of delight, by any new men of the woods, whose services were required over fresh hunting grounds. The prints of a panther are rounder than a tiger's, especially about the toes, which are almost circular, while the tiger's toemark rather resembles the human great toe. Hyænas' footprints may for the moment be mistaken for the panther's, but signs of the nails, as in the case of a large dog or wolf, will be seen wherever the ground is at all soft or dusty, whereas all the cats from the tiger downwards show no such nailmarks, merely the round ball of the toes. "Marg" or "punja" was the term for footprints in these districts, but it would vary in many others. Hunting is very silent work, so fortunately one does not have to acquire very many new words on changing to distant camps.

Now comes the worst part of the whole hunt, for unless a good or lucky shot has left the tiger dead on the spot, it must be followed up until again found either dead or alive. These kills dead at once will be seldom, about one in every five cases, which is not to be wondered at, for the tigers that by creeping slowly past the gunner give him the chance of settling them at once will be in about that proportion; the rest, racing by in long bounds or dodging quickly among the thick bushes, affording a mere glimpse to fire at, will get away far ahead, more or less wounded only.

The first thing on the body of beaters coming up is to

look for blood where the tiger was last seen; this found the procession for following up will be formed most carefully. There is no need to be in any great hurry about starting, for the little time spent in a smoke all round for the men will refresh them, and give the wounded brute more chance of bleeding to death or of becoming very feeble. At length all being ready a start is made with the "band" in the rear, but keeping close behind the rest of the men, and making a noise or not as deemed fit. The sportsmen head the procession with rifles at the "ready," keeping guard over the one or more trackers stooping low down while engaged in carefully looking for each footprint or the faintest speck of blood sprinkled over the high grass or bushes around, which clearly denote the direction the wounded game has taken. Behind the hunters are the men most to be trusted, carrying the spare guns (muzzles well up), which they will pass without the least flurry or delay to the sportsmen the moment they may be required in exchange for empty rifles just fired at the again-found wounded beast.

Next to these gun carriers, who now-a-days would hardly be required, for thanks to breach loaders one can get the same empty gun ready again in almost less time than it could be exchanged for another, are other men carrying a good supply of stones. These they will by order from time to time fling into any likely-looking lurking place that may be pointed out, such as extra dense bushes, green patches of reeds that may be met with as the whole party advances at a very careful foot's pace, shouting or making as much noise as may be required.

There is not much danger to any one engaged in thus carefully following up a wounded tiger, for to avoid such a mass of men and noise the animal will move off as far as it can possibly go, frequently falling dead while so exerting itself to escape. There is seldom need to follow very far in this manner; a few hundred yards will be pretty sure to either end in the party coming upon the dead tiger, or else they will discover from his angry growls or roaring the particular bush or rocky place he has chosen to lie up in, being most probably too faint to travel farther. Men from behind will now, by climbing any trees near at hand, or high overlooking rocks, be, most likely, able to get a view of the beast, and so point out the exact spot where it is hiding, when it can be successfully shot dead, or by a shower of stones, or a bullet fired at guess, be induced to show itself clearly, when the same result will follow.

Sometimes the tiger will make an attempt to charge out of his hiding-place on being so disturbed, in the desperate hope of scattering his enemies, but on finding the compact body of men and the terrible noise he has to face, is almost certain to turn off or stop short after coming on a few yards forward with most alarming roars and seemingly desperate determination. Any such move on his part will generally give the required chance for fair open shooting, which soon finishes him in his already crippled state.

While thus following up the wounded animal, the trackers will often be able to tell exactly where and how badly it is wounded, the marks of the blood on grass and bushes showing how high up the wound may be on its body, also whether the ball has gone clean through. This will be clearly seen by the squirting out of the blood on both sides, and so leaving double traces of the beast's course. Very rarely indeed will any wounded game escape when thus carefully looked for. If it does the wound will certainly be either a very slight one, or most probably a shot in the stomach only. This will soon be known, for little or no blood follows such a very bad hit, though the animal will eventually die from it; but then the skin will be lost, or have become so tainted, even if recovered, as to be not worth preserving.

Having thus described the usual method of looking on speculation for big game in the ravines and hillsides of this country, often beating four or more likely places in one day's work, a selection of anecdotes from the "Tiger Book of 1857" shall be made as further exemplifying the sport, though the following are the adventures of a griffin or novice at tiger hunting.

Some people seem to imagine that "big game" has become rather scarce of late years, but it is doubtful if a third part of the vast mountainous jungle tracts of India have ever been trodden by European feet. Moral: do not waste time and labour hunting over old cleared off ground, but ever try farther afield over fresh undisturbed districts (all due inquiry of course having been previously made).

CHAPTER X.

TIGER SHOOTING.

ADVENTURES OF A NEW HAND—CAUTIONS TO BEGINNERS—AVOIDABLE ACCIDENTS —CATTLE KILLING—REVENGE.

HAVING heard there was a tiger at the village of "Bahara," thirteen miles from camp, after looking in vain for it all day I determined to sit up, in the hope of getting a shot by moonlight, on being assured that the tiger invariably came to drink at a lake close to the village. As a bait a half-starved bullock was tied up by the horns to the trunk of a small tamarind tree, while I got into another such tree close by, sitting on some boughs cut down and placed crosswise, taking with me three double guns. After watching some time the moon went down, when finding it too dark to distinguish any object I let down the three guns to the foot of the tree and prepared to descend. No sooner had my feet touched the ground than an awful roar from a bush not a dozen paces off made me nearly jump out of my skin! Instantly seizing a gun, I blazed away at random both barrels in the hope that the tiger would take the hint and disperse, but to my horror he only repeated the loud "wough," so after firing the remaining four barrels into the bush without being able to see anything, I raced off at best pace towards the village. Here to my joy I met some men hastening towards me. They had been waiting to hear the shot that should announce the tiger's death, but now concluded from the repeated shots and the loud roars that of course the tiger had been killed. After undeceiving them they agreed to return with me to recover the guns and release the bullock, but just as we had hastily picked up the guns another roar close by caused us all to run off at top speed.

After passing the night under a tree close to the village where my horse and man were waiting, we went early next morning to look for the bullock, but found it killed and half eaten. Being obliged to be back in camp early, there was no time to hunt up the gorged tiger, perhaps still close by, as the villagers much wished. All my shots must have missed, being fired too high in the dark, and the tiger merely roared to get rid of self and men. Before getting out of the tree I noticed the bullock was very restless and made violent efforts to get free, doubtless having seen or smelt the tiger, but at the time I concluded it was merely like myself, only tired of waiting so long in one place. This case cured me of night watching, most unsatisfactory work at the best, and very seldom successful.

Here is another instance of the luck that seems to attend griffins in hunting, as if to encourage or lead them on at the noble art. After thus losing a bear, I mounted my horse and rode slowly across country towards the tent, taking with me two Bheels, a single-barrel rifle, and my large dog "Wull," a queer bred one between an English bulldog and Persian greyhound, named Vulcan, but corrupted as above by the natives. Presently we came upon two travellers, who to our surprise began to call out loudly and seemed much frightened. They declared to having seen a large tiger lying down near the roadside, and pointed in the direction it had just gone off. Hoping to get a distant shot at the brute, I quickly dismounted and went after it.

On going up to a large bush about sixty yards off, to my astonishment out jumped the tiger from the opposite side, and in a few bounds made across the dry bed of a river that was close by. Directly "Wull" saw the tiger (which he no doubt mistook for some new sort of deer), he left my heels and set off after it, giving tongue all the while, and keeping close behind the brute. In vain I whistled and called back the dog, for presently we heard him evidently baying the tiger among some high green reeds on the opposite bank of the river.

Suddenly one of the Bheels who had followed me called out that the tiger was coming back, and instantly ran off in the surrounding thick jungle. I looked up and saw the tiger coming down the bank straight towards me closely followed by the dog, still barking loudly. The beast had nearly recrossed the river in a few long bounds, and was within thirty paces, when I jerked up the rifle and fired. Then flinging down the empty gun, I dived among the thorn bushes, taking in my headlong flight the same course the Bheel had done before me, for while jumping across some deep broken rocks I passed this man, who had missed his footing and fallen to the bottom. This Bheel soon came limping up and joined me with the two travellers, in whose charge the horse had been left. While assuring them that I felt sure the tiger was hit, for he threw up his head in the air on my firing, a crashing and panting noise was heard among the bushes close by. This caused another panic, but as we ran off in all directions some one called out it was only the dog, so the alarm was soon over.

After debating some time, the two Bheels agreed to return with me to recover the rifle. Very cautiously we went, half expecting to meet the tiger at every step. At length I found and quickly reloaded the rifle, and then, feeling more safe, advanced to see if there was any blood about the spot where I had fired at the tiger, when, after going a dozen yards or so, to our great delight and astonishment we saw it lying quite dead among some low willow bushes in the river's bed. It had been killed by the veriest accident, for the bullet, without entering the skull, had merely grazed the extreme top of the head, leaving a long wound more like the cut from an axe than any shot hole. This tiger measured eleven feet eleven inches, and was very stout.

Strange to tell, my old horse did not show any signs of fear on being taken up to the tiger, but coolly smelt it over, though but just killed and quite warm. The men thought this beast must have heard the horse's footsteps and was waiting for it when so luckily disturbed by the two travellers, while the dog by its loud barking had evidently confused the brute and turned it back on us. We skinned the tiger on the spot.

The following few scenes occurred in company with my friend A. B. L.:—

While passing through this village "Koree," and waiting for the camels and kit to come up, L. and self started to see if any signs of big game could be found, taking merely a double gun each. We persuaded two Bheels and a lad to accompany us and point out the most likely ground. Scarcely had we gone a few hundred yards from the village when, while walking through a date grove, I saw a tigress reclining in the shade of a small palm tree, certainly not more than ten paces distant. It appeared to be dozing during the great heat of the day, and lazily turned round its head merely to look at us. This gave me time to take good aim and quickly send a ball through its skull, which was followed up by two shots in the chest from my friend's gun. These shots doubled up the tigress in a heap and it fell over dead without a groan. Directly the men with us caught sight of what we were firing at they sprang up the first trees at hand, nor could we persuade them to descend until we had pulled out the tigress by its hind legs from under the low shady palm tree, so astonished did they seem at the whole proceeding.

Next day at the nearest village, "Chuldoo," three miles off, a tiger was seen by our scouts to enter a date grove close under the village walls. After a long search, very silently conducted, part of the tiger could be seen, but it was impossible to tell whether it was lying head or tail foremost, merely a patch of the bright skin being visible, so after placing all the spare guns in front on the ground and having sent the men away to a safe distance, we knelt down within twelve yards of the brute and fired a volley into it. Up jumped the tiger and, luckily for us, crashed off through the thick jungle in the opposite direction. The men were recalled and the blood marks followed, when we soon came on the tiger quite dead.

Shortly afterwards, at another village, "Deypoora," near this, we heard of a tiger that had killed several bullocks, and was said to live out in the open plain, under some rocks. Quietly going to this spot, on tip-toe, and looking down over the edge of the rock, there was the tiger, stretched out at full length, just three yards below; he looked up and grinned at us horribly, when we each gave him a bullet; whereupon he sprang into some dense bushes close by, before even a second shot could be fired. On going down we found some spots of blood, and easily took these on to a steep, stony ravine, when they suddenly ceased. The ground was bare sheet rock, so no foot-prints could be found. Presently a herd of goats came by grazing most unconcernedly, so no tiger could have passed them. We now retraced our steps, when a Bheel silently pointed to a cave, formed by a large ledge of rock that had fallen from above, and which we had already passed close by. We knew his meaning, but there was an awkward, steep bank behind us, so we could only get a peep inside the cave, from about four yards off;

however all the guns were silently handed down to us, and the men went back to a safe distance. On kneeling down, side by side, all that could be seen within the dark cave was the indistinct outline of the tiger's head, but its two eyes were shining very clearly. We agreed, in a whisper, to fire together—at the word "one, two, three," being given in a very low tone by myself. On the smoke clearing away, we were delighted to see the foe stretched out stiff on its back, the white of the stomach being uppermost, and very visible.

On going closer, two small holes, one over each eyebrow, from which streams of blood trickled down, caused us to congratulate each other on our good aim at the tiger's head. We could now see that the cave was very spacious inside, although it had but a very small entrance.

While talking over our lucky shots, I observed one of the tiger's arms move slightly, but as if from mere muscular action, and suggested firing another shot to make sure, but on L. objecting that it was unnecessarily spoiling the skin, I agreed to fire where our knives would be first used in taking off the tiger's skin, so fired the remaining barrel without putting the gun to my shoulder, into the beast's chest. All this time the men, seeing us so close to the cave, came running up in great delight, thinking that their enemy must be dead, as we also most certainly did; but no sooner had I fired, than, with a frightful roar, up jumped the tiger, as lively as ever! My friend sprang up on the high rock, and kept guard, with his remaining barrel loaded, while I rushed back among the men, who were crowded round, upsetting three or four and myself in so doing. For a moment there was a terrible panic; the ground being so uneven and stony, many men fell over and tripped up each other. Some got up trees, others ran out of sight. All this time the tiger never left off roaring; and I fully thought he was outside the cave, killing each man as he caught them; instead of which, being much confused, he luckily remained inside the den, round and round which he kept walking, seemingly without being able to find his way out. At last I got up, and snatched a loaded gun lying with the rest of our battery on the ground, and then climbed up a small tree just in front of the cave. There were two men already in this low tree, so the branches were bent down unpleasantly close to the ground with our weight. Here I fired twelve more shots, at as many paces distance, into this tiger, before he was quiet. Only its fore arm and the lower part of its body could be hit, every time he came round or appeared at the mouth of the cave.

At last, all being still, we came down from our posts, and this time found the tiger really dead—riddled with bullets. The place was covered with guns, drums, bows, spears, shoes, &c., and some of the men much bruised by their falls. It seemed our first two shots had merely stunned the tiger, missing the brain. The shot in the chest most effectually revived him.

This was a truly wonderful escape for every one concerned, for, supposing the tiger dead, we should have begun to haul him out of the cave, and skin him on the spot, when, no doubt, the knives would have revived him, and the consequences been awful! for the men on these occasions crowd round to assist in the skinning operation, and discuss the tiger's misdeeds while living. Doubtless several lives would have been lost! This was a caution, indeed, never to fear making a few extra holes in a skin to be quite sure of a "kill." The tiger was a very large old one. This next shows how, with the same friend, the "Jaat" man-eater was killed.

On arriving at "Jaat" we collected as many men as possible overnight, intending to have another try for our old enemy, the man-eating tiger, still the terror of the neighbourhood. Our plan was of starting at first break of day to try and cut off the tiger from its retreat among the disused iron pits, where it used to lie concealed during the daytime. These men were told to spread themselves out over a large extent of open country, and beat towards the iron pits, over which we kept guard. There was no danger at this cool time of the morning in thus separating the beaters, for we knew the tiger would make direct for its old refuge, the iron pits, on being disturbed; as really happened, for scarcely had we heard the first faint sounds of the drums and pistol shots, when we saw, to our delight, the tiger coming from a long way off straight to our post. We let her come, at a jog trot, within ten yards, when both the rifles fired together, dropped the beast, and another shot or two killed it. Great was the excitement of the people on hearing of our good luck; men at once ran off with the news, and the populace turned out to meet the tiger's body, which was carried in triumph on small trees, hastily cut down, to our tent. There was no mistaking this brute for the real man-eater for no further casualties occurred, although during the two years previous to its death over forty people of this town had been killed and carried off by this tigress. It measured ten feet and a few inches long. The tusks were, from some cause or accident, quite worn down, but the animal was very fat, and seemed in full vigour, with bright glossy coat, contrary to the general idea that man-eating tigers are invariably thin, worn-out, and mangy animals; but, owing to its broken or deficient teeth, she may have found killing human beings easier work than cattle or deer slaying.

Next day the prints of a large tiger were found leading into a very deep, wide ravine, so we started to beat it. Just after taking up our position on a steep bank, half-way down the side of the ravine, we were startled by a stone falling from above, close to us, and, on looking up, a fine panther was seen moving on just above, so we were obliged to fire, though after nobler game. We gave the brute four shots, on which it bounded down a small branch of the big ravine we were guarding. Thinking the panther was trying to make off, I ran after it with a spare gun for a parting shot, when, to my astonishment, I saw the beast in the act of charging straight down hill from directly overhead. Stopping short, I fired both barrels quite close into the panther, and then, to save being sprung upon, jumped off the rocky ledge on which we were standing into a small tree below; L. seeing me fire, got ready instantly, and, with a famous shot in the head, rolled over the panther while in the very act of leaping down from above after me, so that it came tumbling through the boughs, doubled up, and fell dead below the tree. L. was only four paces off when making this very lucky shot, that, no doubt, saved me from a severe mauling at least. The panther was well riddled with bullets, but they did not stop its charge in the least.

Hearing our shots, the men thought we had turned out the big tiger alone, so left off beating; but by signs we signalled them to continue their noise, when soon the old tiger was seen ascending the opposite side of the wide ravine, just in front of our post, when four rifle shots, as it bounded up the steep bank, luckily rolled it over, at quite ninety yards distance. It came down, roaring and biting at every small tree-trunk, having had its back broken by a bullet. Soon it stopped rolling down, when it was shot dead, while clawing at each bush and big stone in reach. This tiger measured eleven feet eleven inches long, and was extremely stout, with an enormous head, being evidently very old. After disembowelling both brutes, they were carried by relays of the men to our tent, and there skinned.

Our good luck seemed to greatly impress the people. A tiger like this will require, at the least, twelve strong men to lift it on the poles. One stout sapling was passed through both the fore paws, tied together, also the hind feet, similarly bound, while two cross strong bars supported this long pole in the middle, or at either end. The men would constantly have to be relieved by relays, while staggering under this heavy load, for the weight of a tiger is something enormous, and quite inconceivable to strangers.

Having heard of bullocks being lately killed at "Doraee" village, six miles off, we started very early for that place, sending on the Jaat men and our guns, and then riding to overtake them. Here we were told of two tigers being in a deep ravine, which turned out to have very little cover in it, and its sides were bare, rocky walls; so to avoid being seen, we had to place ourselves in some low, thick willow bushes, in the very middle of this ravine, or bed of a river rather, a bad, risky position to take up, but there was no other shelter about. Soon after the beat began, a tigress came slowly on, but, on being fired at, raced past us so quickly that there was not time to exchange the empty rifles for other guns. She went by very close, roaring awfully, but was badly wounded, we knew. Just as we had reloaded, a very large tiger was seen coming on down the middle of the ravine, when about twenty paces off he pulled up and stood, staring hard at our hunting caps and faces, for nothing else was visible above the thick willow bushes. Being quite ready for him, we fired together, when the tiger, instead of charging forward, luckily began bounding about on all sides. This confused conduct gave us capital chances of finishing him with more shots, when he was killed far easier than, from his great size, seemed likely to be the case. This tiger measured over eleven feet, and was very broad, with long curly locks about the face, and quite a short mane down the back of the neck, more so than in any other tigers seen in Rajpootana—a noble appearance.

The first wounded tigress had now to be looked for, so the procession was formed, and some very thick thorny cover passed through, when we were recalled, a man having discovered the tigress after we had passed it by. It took some little time to make this animal out, for it was lying flat, almost covered with leaves, and merely the heaving of its sides showed where it was, in the dark, thick undergrowth of this dense jungle. We all stood close together in a compact body, and then fired at about eight paces distance. Up jumped the tigress, with a bound forward, and terrible roars, causing a temporary panic, as every one involuntarily stepped back a pace, and in so doing tumbled over his neighbour. Luckily the beast again crouched down, being too weak to come on, or else stopped by the thick thorn bushes. Another advance together was made, and more shots poured in, when the "kill" was secured. The brushwood had to be cut down by the men's axes, and a lane cleared before this tigress could be got out from under the thick bushes.

It was dark before we had finished skinning and pegging down these two tigers—a long day's work, and one luckily ended. The big tiger had killed and gorged himself over a full-grown camel the day before, but would not allow the tigress to touch it, for she was quite empty, though from their footprints we could see these two animals had been living together some days before—very ungallant conduct! We several times observed on future occasions that a very large old monster tiger was far easier to kill than a younger one; a few shots generally being sufficient for the big tigers, while the others would take far more lead, and be lively for a much longer time.

An officer, in charge of these districts, told me that he had once been kept awake nearly all night by the awful row two tigers were making near his tent, while travelling in this part of the country. Next morning it appeared that a large buffalo had been killed by a tiger, which is sure to be the work of a very old, strong tiger. Near the defunct buffalo an immense male tiger was also found dead, with many claw and teeth marks deeply scored upon him, and after the people had followed some blood spots, a little way off, they came upon another monster tiger, also dead, and scored all over, like the first, with teeth and claw wounds. These two old brutes had contrived to kill each other somehow, like the Kilkenny cats! but the buffalo was hardly touched, or uneaten.

Another instance was told me by a friend of a tiger having been discovered eating the carcase of a dead bear that had been shot, and left skinned in the woods, some two days previously. A most extraordinary case, but not unknown, among both tigers and panthers, as far as feasting on animals not fresh killed by themselves is concerned. I have also seen where these beasts have gnawn the fallen, decaying trunks of dead trees in a phosphorescent state, but that was considered to be more for a taste of the salt wood than from hunger, for other brutes—such as wolves, hyænas, wild dogs, will also gnaw these fallen trees, leaving the marks of their teeth quite plain on the soft, pulpy, rotten wood.

On the morning following our last "kill," the men reported having found the fresh prints of two more tigers in a thick cover not far off, on the banks of a wide stream; so, with the "band" and other beaters, we started to look them up. After driving the river-banks for a long way, until the country became quite bare and open, no tigers appeared, so, thinking they might be hiding, very close, in the dense corinda bushes that bordered this stream, I determined to walk back down the bed of the river, and have a good look under each bush. After going some distance in this manner, with my rifle at the "ready," and wading in water waist high, while peering under a large corinda bush, so shady, that all beneath appeared quite dark, I thought something like a tiger's form could be distinguished, so waded to the opposite bank, and arranged with L. to fire a volley on speculation into this bush. First the men were all collected, and sent back as usual to a safe distance, except one left up a high tree close by to look out. The spare guns being placed all ready at our feet, we fired four shots, when there was some movement in the big bush, and on more shots being given, a tiger showed itself, but was instantly dropped dead by a shot in the head, the body rolling half down the sloping bank, and resting partly in the water.

Thinking, after this fusilade, that all must be over, the men crossed over by a ford, and were standing collected round this dead tiger on the bank above, talking over its death, pointing out the shot-holes, and discussing the mischief it had done to their cattle, as is the custom in these cases, when suddenly a terrific roar was heard from the very midst of the crowd, as it appeared. Instantly there was a terrible panic, many leaping, with a great splash, into the water, and struggling to get across, in the utmost terror. On hearing this roar, well knowing there must be another tiger close by, and all the guns unloaded, we each looked out for our own safety. L. dived under a thick bush, while I sprang up a small tree close at hand, my costume at the time being very scanty, merely a brown shirt on, for, feeling chilled after wading so long while searching down the stream, all my other clothes had been spread out in the sun to dry. Presently, the cry arose that a man had been killed.

The panic all round being now over, the guns were quickly reloaded, and, on going to the spot, we found the man who had been placed on the look-out had met with a most narrow escape. Without orders, he had come down from his tree, and was running to join his companions in looking at the dead tiger, when suddenly another tiger rushed out at him from the very bush round which the crowd were standing, upsetting him in its flight, and clawing off his thick turban, which, no doubt, greatly helped to save him, for merely a few deep scratches were inflicted while being thus scampered over. It then appeared there was another tiger all the time in the bush, but so long as the men kept close together it did not dare to attack any one, though they were only two yards from where this beast was lying hid, but on seeing this single man approach, he was at once charged and rolled over by the retreating tiger. The wounded man was carried to the nearest village, not much hurt, when plenty of opium, the usual remedy in these cases, soon quieted him, and he soon recovered. There was much diving and searching in the river for shoes, shields, swords, spears, and other articles lost in the panic.

We had another hunt for the escaped tiger, and got some long shots at it as it made off at a canter for some hills close by. Next morning another tiger was reported in the same cover as yesterday, and on shooting it, we found it was the same beast that had got clear off the day before, for it had one of our bullet wounds in the stomach, the hair round this shot-hole being licked off and turned back, wet from the tiger's tongue. No doubt it had returned to look for its dead companion. Wounds were often observed to be so licked by tigers, to allay the pain, most likely. A tiger's tongue is very rough, with a number of short strong prickles covering it, all lying backwards; with these every scrap of meat can be scraped off bones in feeding.

Just such another accident befell one of our beaters, and serves to show the necessity for all keeping in a compact, close body while looking for tigers. This man had lost several of his cattle, and being very angry at not being able to make a tiger leave a dense cover it had sought shelter in, at last persisted, in spite of the most urgent warnings and persuasions of the other beaters, in rushing down, sword in hand, into the thick patch of jungle. The tiger at once knocked him over, and then crept still further back into the dark, close bushes. The rest of the men then, in a body, rushed on and brought out their wounded comrade. We were some distance off at the time, but could hear the combined roaring and yells of the tiger and men. Next day the tiger was shot, and the wounded man luckily soon recovered.

These accidents are very distressing at the time, and most vexing, when one feels that a little precaution might prevent them altogether. No other harm ever befell any of my men at this supposed most dangerous work, except to a friend, which will be explained further on.

On two occasions tigers have charged down on me, so close that the hair of one's chest was singed by the gun, the flash luckily causing the brute to turn off on one side and pass on. The other tiger fell dead only two yards off in front, shot through the head, fortunately. These shaves happen to most hunters, and even worse, showing the necessity for always being prepared with the rifle in hand, and pretty quick too in using it.

Wild boars—big, savage, solitary fellows—are apt to charge out on the passing hunter. Two or three times, on hearing the men behind call out, I have been only just in time, by wheeling sharp round and blazing into the pork, to save the chance of being ripped. Once, while snipe shooting, I so killed a big boar with No. 8 shot, firing both barrels into his ribs as he raced by, on my jumping aside, not above two paces off; he bolted out of some high, dry reeds on the edge of a swamp. Thinking no more of the matter, I had gone on shooting, when, about one hundred yards or more ahead, the pig was found dead in some rushes, with two big holes, close together, blown in his side. It is not always easy to keep the men properly close together, so as to render the danger as slight as possible of hunting up big game on foot.

I once lost a very fine tiger by the carelessness of two men, who left their party to go down to drink at a river, along the banks of which this tiger had been carefully and nicely driven for some long way, when suddenly there was a tremendous roar, which was continued as this beast bolted back past the gang of beaters and "band." Men on the look-out above saw this tiger regularly stalk these two fools, and were luckily able to warn them in time, when they both jumped down into the river, and the tiger raced back. This was a very knowing old tiger, well known and much hated, for he used to kill buffaloes in broad day close to a village, and had been often hunted by natives. I was well placed on a large boulder rock, ten feet high, and must have killed the brute, for it could be seen from above coming on famously.

At another time, there was a painful suspense. At the very end of a cover, in the bed of a river, a tiger suddenly bolted back past the beaters, with the usual amount of roaring, then all was still. Soon, a good deal of shouting and calling out of names was heard, this noise being continued, in most anxious tones, for some time. I left my post to see what was the matter, when it appeared a lazy fellow had stopped behind to smoke his pipe, without informing any one of his intention. As he came sauntering up, there was great rejoicing, mingled with a desire to kick him for the anxiety he had caused so needlessly, for all thought the tiger must have carried him off from the midst of the men. There was a large open space in this cover, across which this tiger objected to pass.

It is often difficult to decide how to beat these scattered covers, or very small patches of jungle. If too long a drive is attempted, the animal gets tired of walking forward so far over the hot ground, or suspects danger, and then insists on breaking back past the men, always a dangerous proceeding; but if too short a drive is tried, then the tiger, who may be lying up in a patch of cover just beyond the hunter's post, on hearing the noise of the beaters, starts off at once, and so escapes all chance of being fired at, or seen even. If there are more than two sportsmen engaged, it is a good plan for one of them to accompany the men. This always insures a first-rate drive, and gives great confidence to all concerned. Choice of position, and this sort of arrangement is always decided at the last moment, by lot, pulling straws for the purpose, soon silently settles the matter.

With regard to buffaloes, the *bœuf a l'eau*, or "water ox," is mostly tiger proof, for, as a rule, only young, half-grown ones are found to be killed, and still smaller ones, calves almost, are used for tying up as tiger baits. Yet an old, full-grown one is occasionally killed, but this is always the act of some immense male tiger, who is at once named as the culprit. Buffaloes, in herds, are fearlessly driven in to graze over swampy bits of jungle, well known to be frequented by tigers, their herdsmen and boys often riding on the buffaloes' backs into the midst of these dangerous looking places, feeling quite safe in the protection afforded by their cattle. Once only was a lad so guarding buffaloes reported to have been carried off by a man-eating tiger.

Having once lost all trace of a wounded tiger that had entered a most dense patch of jungle in the bed of a river, where it was impossible to see even a yard ahead, I was puzzled what to suggest, when a drove of cattle, including several buffaloes, came past, so the men turned these animals into the cover, where the last drops of the tiger's blood were to be seen; presently there was a terrific row among the buffaloes, who began snorting and crashing through the long grass and bushes, with loud bellowing, and at last they set to fighting among themselves in a desperate manner, caused by their smelling the tiger's blood, which seemed to have the effect of most decidedly getting up their own. Following, at length, in the wake of these cattle so enraged, we found the tiger had left the cover, or been driven away by the disturbance. On the herdsmen coming up, they had great difficulty in again collecting their buffaloes from out of this thick patch of jungle, vehemently abusing us, but the dodge was worth knowing at a pinch.

Buffaloes are commonly reported, on discovering the tiger's presence, to form a sort of line, and charge down upon him in a body, trampling him under foot, and goring him with their long horns, if not quick enough to get clear away from such obstinate, powerful enemies; but with cows the tiger has it all his own way, for a single loud roar is sufficient to send the largest herd off scampering away, tails up and heads down, in the wildest state of alarm, as I have witnessed on some few occasions. The first time, one unfortunate cow was left behind, with a broken leg, being upset by its fellows in the confusion.

Tigers know well enough where cattle are to be found, either on being driven out to graze, or on returning home towards evening, so he will lurk in the long grass, and suddenly start up, seizing the bullock by its head, neck, or shoulder, with his immensely powerful arms, claws well out; the ox is felled or dragged down to the ground, at the same time having its neck dislocated by the wrench as it is thrown over. This attack is not always successful, for I have seen oxen that had somehow managed to escape the tiger's clutches, after being scored about the neck and shoulders with long, deep wide-spread gashes, though these lucky escapes are very rare indeed. The moment the bullock is seized, there is a sudden stampede or short rush on all sides of the rest of the herd, which tells only too plainly what has happened. Several men have told me they have witnessed a "kill" of cattle, but the affair seems to be so very sudden, and there is so much confusion at the moment, that no precise description was to be obtained, beyond that it was more of a wrestling match than any charging or far-springing attack.

Being left in possession of his prey, the tiger will lie up in some thick bush close by, keeping watch over it, or if killed in too open a spot, he may even drag the carcase some little distance to any more convenient sheltered place, waiting close by in hiding until about sunset, when he will stealthily creep out to dine, invariably beginning at the victim's rump or hind quarters, and so eating upwards, about a third or less of the body, frequently going off to drink at the nearest piece of water, and somehow there always does happen to be water near a "kill," as if the spot were selected on purpose.

Now is the time chosen by the cattle owner, or some friend with a matchlock, to have his revenge. Hastily forming a sort of platform of cut boughs, or bamboos tied together crosswise, or better still, firmly fastening a native cot up in the branches of some good high tree standing near where the dead bullock's body has been left by the tiger, the matchlock man, shortly before sunset, will climb up the tree, and, sitting patiently and quite silent, in the cot or platform around which some green twigs have been fastened (or the small boughs of the tree have been bent down and interwoven so as to make a screen for the perfect concealment of the marksman), will await his chance of a fair shot at the tiger as it creeps out to feed on the dead ox. Sometimes no tiger will appear, having either smelt the lighted match of the gun, or become otherwise aware of the man's presence, or it has suspected some such trap. Natives manage to kill a good many tigers in this manner, but they frequently merely wound them, owing chiefly to the very inferior gunpowder used (for the country-made gunpowder is coarse and bad in the extreme), also to the very small bullet used in matchlocks, for it was a common occurrence on skinning both bears and tigers to find these small, half-flattened balls just under the skin, mostly on the back parts.

The bears get fired at by men watching their fields of ripening grain from high stands or platforms built for the purpose, in the middle of these fields, on which the villagers pass the whole night, to scare away hog, deer, nil-ghai, &c., that come in herds to rob the corn. Twice only have I been induced to thus watch for two particularly knowing tigers, that could not be found or tracked down anywhere, both times unsuccessfully. Nothing can be more unsatisfactory, the cramped position and uncertainty making the whole business anything but a pleasure. Still it is frequently done, when there is no other hope or means of finding a tiger, as in some vast forest, where it is hardly possible to look up the brute. The gunner in this, as in all other cases of waiting in ambush, had best be alone, for if he has a native companion to help keep watch, there will, to a perfect certainty, be some mishap or other to scare away the game, most unintentional, no doubt, but nevertheless certain to occur—an unlucky sneeze, cough, or movement of some kind, being the chief causes. A perfectly trained Shikaree might be the exception to this rule.

An old cowherd once showed me how he had managed to cry quits with the tigers that had killed many of his cattle. Knowing that the bullocks thighs and hind quarters are the parts to be invariably first eaten, he had cut long, deep gashes close together with his knife, and rubbed in a quantity of powdered arsenic well into these cuts of each fresh-killed ox, and then left the carcase. With each mouthful of meat the tiger insensibly swallows a quantity of this poison, which soon creates such excessive thirst that it drinks, and drinks, till it falls dead by the water. This man had a good supply of arsenic in a wallet worn round his waist. There is another common berry in the woods that answers just as well for poison, being tasteless. I was shown the remains of three dead tigers, killed in this manner, at three separate pools of water within a circuit of as many miles.

If wounded by the matchlock ball, there is a good chance of the animal dying, sooner or later, from the effects of maggots, which are almost sure to be bred in the wound, owing to the swarms of flies everywhere about. Very seldom tigers are met with that have recovered from the bullets of English rifles, the balls being so much larger, and fired with so much greater force; still two such cases did come under my knowledge, one such tiger being lame, and particularly knowing in consequence.

CHAPTER XI.

TIGER SHOOTING.

TIGER'S VOICE—OLD JACKALS—JUNGLE ENCAMPMENT—SKINNING—PEGGING DOWN—TIGER'S AGE.

WHILE camping out in the woods one is often made aware of the fact that tigers are in the neighbourhood by hearing them call, towards dusk of an evening, and generally from some high ground. The noise is then a peculiar grunting sound, very different from the usual mere "wough," or loud, angry, prolonged roar, uttered from some place they object to be turned out of, or moved from, if wounded. This evening call is a succession of very deep-toned, hollow-voiced, loud grunts, sounding like "hough-hough!" "hough-hough!" "hough-hough!" seldom more than four, six, or eight of these double grunts, uttered with a very short or no interval between each bellow, or call, are made at a time. Then all is still; but presently the self-same row, or another set of such calls, is heard in another direction, at some further distance, and is most likely repeated still farther off in some other quarter.

This may be either a challenge or calling to one another, or, as is supposed, with the object of startling deer and other prey into some other spot, where they may be afterwards silently pounced upon, after having been thus driven in the required direction from several points. The tiger will often make this noise, too, in the very early dawn, before retiring to rest for the day, after its night's long prowl. Panthers, also, call sometimes even during the day, but the voice is very different, not being so loud, and of a more prolonged howl.

Tigers have two, three, and even four cubs at a birth, but at no stated time of the year, though it seemed to be generally just before the rains set in, for there were several long, deep, wide caves about, that the men seemed very shy of approaching, stating that tigresses were often known to have their cubs in them. Once, two cubs were found close to the walls of a village in a ravine filled with a thick cactus sort of jungle; these cubs could be heard calling to the mother from the village, their den being not more than thirty yards distant. It only shows how little these brutes fear men when not molested, for nobody seemed to think of disturbing this tigress and her family. There appeared to be about two tigresses to every male tiger, judging by the sex of those killed; but this apparent disproportion may be accounted for by the fact that the big tiger will surely kill any young male cub he may meet with, if possible, as the Bheels confidently asserted was the case. The young tigresses kept with the mothers until nearly full grown, while the young male would be always met with alone; for when about half-grown, or rather more, after having been shown by its mother how to kill game, it was left to shift for itself.

At first nothing comes amiss to these cubs, from peacocks upwards. Having shot a tigress, at one village, that was known to have left her cubs somewhere, we shortly afterwards heard that on these small tigers, in a starving state, no doubt, having attempted to kill some goats, the people rose in a body, drove the cubs into a cave, and there roasted them by a bonfire of grass and dry sticks, with which the cave was filled. These people imitated the cries of these suffocated innocents, and seemed to think the affair a good joke. Tiger cubs are sometimes brought in for sale when about a month old, being found in caves or high grass, but they are difficult to rear in confinement, being subject to a sort of paralysis in the loins or hind quarters that soon kills them.

Returning silently homewards with my men one evening, we came upon a large tiger, busily engaged in knocking small fish, each about a few inches long only, out of a shallow piece of water, with his broad, open paw; each sprat was lapped up while flopping about on the sheet-rock that formed the bed of a stream, now completely dried up during the hot weather, except at a few shallow, small pools, where these fish, frogs, &c., were collected in a mass. This tiger was shot there and then, before being aware of our presence, by a ball through the head.

On skinning tigers, several times the broken quills of porcupines were found deeply embedded in the paws, arms, and chest-parts, showing that the porcupine had been knocked over by a blow, being, most likely, mistaken for a small pig while wandering about at night, as these animals usually do, while in search of food, such as grain, roots, fruit, &c.

On two occasions a large hyæna and full-grown hunting cheeta were found fresh killed, but otherwise untouched, by a single blow of a tiger's paw, the wide claw-marks being distinctly visible; no doubt these victims had incautiously passed too close to the tiger's lair, and suffered accordingly. In both these cases the bodies were lying near caves on the sides of rocky, hilly ground—rather singular for the hunting cheeta, for they are mostly found in wide, open plains.

Directly after a "kill" of a bullock or samber deer, &c., vultures begin to assemble from all points, being somehow soon aware of the murder, either by sight or sense of smell, which in both senses must be extraordinarily powerful, for perhaps not one of these birds will be in sight before the prey is killed. The theory is, that these vultures are spread singly over an infinite space in the sky, soaring aloft, each in his own extensive, clear circle; but on any one bird moving off and descending earthwards on becoming aware of the death of some quarry or other carrion, all the other vultures quit their stations, and also fly towards the spot indicated. In this manner miles upon miles of ground can be watched from above by a few score birds, with slight chance of anything eatable escaping their notice. Seeing the vultures thus assembling from all quarters, frequently gives the hunter warning of a tiger's whereabouts. Jackals also contrive to be somehow well aware of the "kill," perhaps from observing the vultures' flight, for they too begin to assemble on the spot; but both they and the birds have the good manners to wait till the tiger has first dined. The jackals sit patiently round, at a respectful distance, while the vultures remain perched on any trees close by. After the tiger has left, there is a regular scramble for the remaining portion of the dead animal, the jackals jumping up and chasing away the vultures as they swoop past them in trying to filch some scrap of meat or entrails, but on these curs at length retiring, each, perhaps, with some bone to gnaw at leisure apart, the vultures begin in earnest, soon completely clearing up every shred of meat, leaving the bones beautifully picked, nothing but a heap of chewed grass from the entrails being left to mark the place, while the ground is stamped smooth and muddy all round. After such a feast, the vultures are often so gorged as to be unable to rise or fly away for the time, being only capable of hopping a few steps out of the way.

There is an old solitary jackal called the "kole balloo," which often accompanies the tiger, and may be heard at night and evening, giving a most peculiar, unearthly scream, not to be mistaken for any other animal's voice. This particular jackal is generally supposed to be too old or worn out to get its living by hunting with its fellows, so remains with the tiger, in the hope of sharing in what is left of any prey that is killed by him, and is credited with finding and pointing out these subjects fit for slaughter. These brutes would be often heard close to our encampment, attracted no doubt by the smell of the horses, camels, bullocks, goats, &c., while all at once recognized the "kole balloo's" presence, and felt sure that a tiger also would not be far off.

On one such occasion, after hearing one of these jackals' long, continued cry, a tiger could be seen passing and repassing a small open space, in the bright moonlight, on the banks of a river where our tent was pitched. No clear enough shot could be taken, for the tiger was no sooner seen than it vanished like a ghost among the surrounding dark bushes. More wood was piled on the fires around, for the horses were much alarmed; at length, towards dawn, both tiger and jackal took themselves off, to everyone's delight.

Jackals have wonderfully keen scent, for I have seen one holding on like a bulldog to the throat of a wounded buck cheetal that had just been shot, and which I was following up. This cur must have sprung out on the wounded deer in passing some bush; it was rolled up like a ball, and the buck was swaying his head from side to side, in vain trying to shake off its enemy. On again being shot, the jackal left the dead cheetal, and sneaked off. In this same manner I have seen a jackal following after a wounded black buck across the open plain, the smell of the deer's blood having, no doubt, aroused him while dozing in some bush, as they do during the heat of the day.

Jackals occasionally go mad, and coming into the villages are most dangerous brutes. At times they become quite bare from mange, losing all their hair, but are then met with alone, a horrible sight.

Here are some scenes from the Tiger Book aforesaid of

jungle life in Rajpootana, but applicable to all time and most places.

On determining to change ground to hunt over a fresh part of the country, a very busy scene would take place —striking the small tents, "rowtees," of which we carried two; one for ourselves, and the other for the servants. Ours was more to keep our kit and goods in than to live under, unless heavy rain happened to fall (the so-called "mango showers," frequent in the hot weather), for we always preferred sleeping and dining out in the open air, and packing up in deal boxes an infinite number of all sorts of articles; these would be divided into equal loads, and placed on the camels' backs. At length, all being ready, mounting our horses, off we started, leaving the dogs and goats to follow of their own accord. First came some men, carrying our guns and the "chagul," or water bag; these acted as guides, to show the way, and were most useful in getting other men at the several villages passed through, or thought worth while halting at, according to the prospect of sport in their neighbourhood. On thus providing their substitutes, we sent them back to their homes, well pleased with a liberal payment, for these men would be of little use over a country with which they were unacquainted; besides, after a very few days' hunting, they seemed anxious to attend to their fields and cattle, so could not stay longer with our party. We rode slowly in advance, looking out for any deer that might be seen, for the pot's sake. Next came the spare horses, led by their grooms, then the camels, following each other in a string, surrounded by our servants, who either rode them or walked. On reaching the halting-ground, the first thing was to select some large shady trees to pitch the tents under, where plenty of good water was near at hand, not neglecting tc see if any bees had formed their nests overhead in the trees, for on more than one occasion, from neglecting or forgetting this precaution we all suffered severely from the bees, that were disturbed by the smoke of our cooking fires Our little encampment was quite picturesque, with the horses picketed in a row, while the servants, bullocks, camels, goats, fowls, and dogs were grouped around, bright wood fires for cooking added to the scene, which ever looked better, in our opinion, when several skins were stretched out and pegged down just before the tents.

This tiresome work, as well as the troublesome one of skinning, or at least of marking out the first cuts in regular order, we always performed, or superintended, assisted by our "Shikarrees," for we found if the business was left to others, great lumps of flesh would be carelessly left on the skins, besides many ugly cuts therein from knives. In like manner the skin would be pegged in any irregular shape, and so spoilt, for skins require to be laid out for pegging down in the most symmetrical manner, great attention being paid that they should retain their proportionate width as well as length. First, for skinning, the cuts extended from between the lower tusks on the lip, straight down the whole length of the animal until the end of the tail, in a perfect line; the upper lip, to between the nostrils, was also slit. Between the fore-arms the skin was cut from the centre of chest or breast-bone to the middle of the foot-pad, each of the toes having its ball slit open, so as to hold a small peg on either side, through the pad or sole parts, thus enabling each foot to be properly spread out, the pad parts being afterwards cut away (on taking up a thoroughly dried skin), for being thick hard substances, they prevented the skins lying properly flat on the ground or floor. In like manner the hind legs would be cut down from the middle of the thighs to the ball of the hind feet, precisely as in the fore legs; great care being taken to make the cuts on each opposite arm or leg exactly resemble the other. The skin round the eyes and ears would be carefully separated from the skull, and close to the bone as possible, the ears being nicely turned down inwards and laid flat before pegging out commenced; if this was neglected (on the skin being taken up), instead of the handsome black velvet-like hair of the ear, with the conspicuous white spot in the centre being shown, merely the coarse brown bare skin of the inside of the ear would appear, an ugly drawback to any tiger-skin looks.

For pegging down, first of all, two stout bamboo pegs should be driven well into the ground, one through each nostril-hole. Each peg is about six or eight inches long, formed of young solid bamboo canes, as thick as one's finger, well pointed with a knife at one end. These pegs were collected from each skin (as it became dry and was taken off the ground), when their points, having been re-sharpened with a knife, they were fit to use over again. A large tiger-skin would take about two hundred pegs or less, each peg being driven in through the edge of the skin, at about half an inch from the margin; if placed too near the edge of the skin they would be apt to tear out when stretching it from either side. Next followed two pegs, one on either side of the upper end or part of the tail next the body. This gave length. The tail-skin, being very thin and brittle, was always left to be pegged down last of all, with the smallest sized pegs too. Then the two fore paws were each stretched out wide, and pegs at the same time driven in them on a level with the ears, the fore feet having some few pegs fastened down to keep them wide open. The hind legs were then pulled out straight and on a line with or square to where the tail joins, their feet being spread wide out and fastened down. Then two men on either side, pulling against each other, and exactly opposite, would each peg down, peg for peg, the respective sides of the animal's arms, sides, and hind legs. The tail, being gently stretched, and

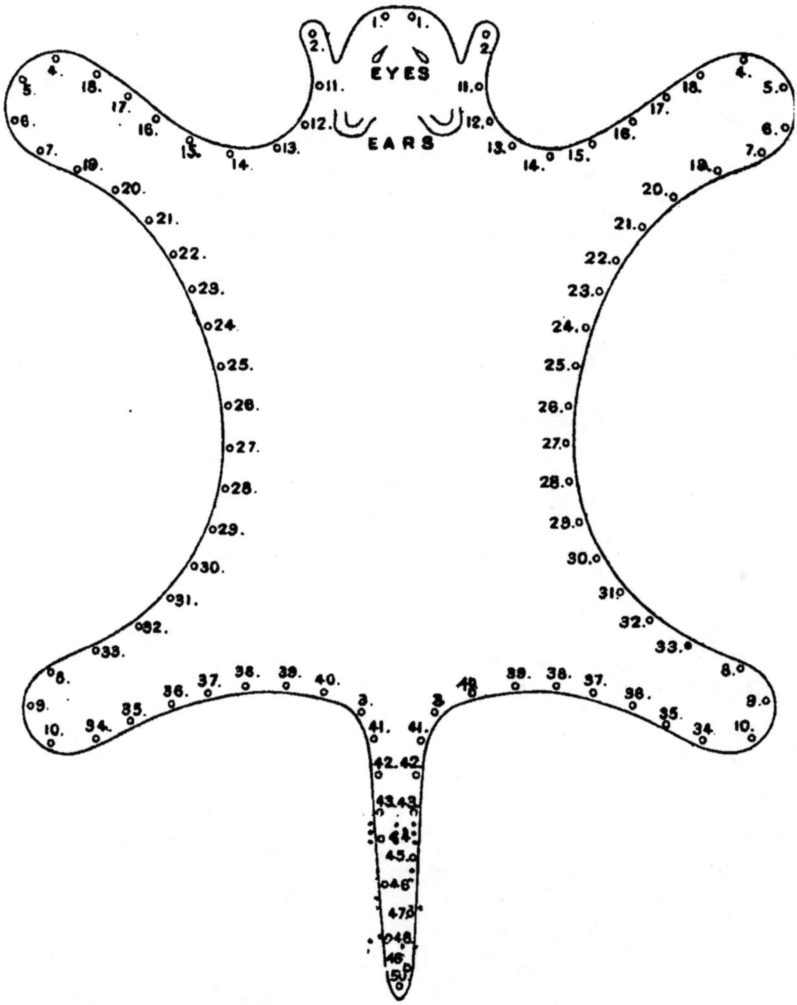

Method of "stretching" and "pegging down" a Tiger Skin, showing the order by number in which the pegs are driven in. Scale: Half-an-inch to a foot.

fastened down with pegs alternately stuck opposite, for it would not be wide enough to admit of two even rows of pegs. So all would at last have an even appearance, with no wrinkles or doubling under of the skin in any part. Sometimes two other men, with the small wooden mallets used for this purpose, would follow each peg as it was at first slightly stuck in the ground, and drive them well down into the earth (where it appeared loose or soft), for skins in afterwards drying are apt to greatly shrink, and can then draw out the pegs in places, spoiling the perfect look or beauty of any skin.

This troublesome job, on doing which well we greatly prided ourselves, did not take long with plenty of hands, but with blunt knives, and bad, broken-ended pegs, many severe raps on the fingers, or cuts even, often happened; however, the trouble was well repaid when at last a coating of arsenical soap, to preserve the skins, had been well rubbed in with long brushes, and we were at leisure to admire our work, and talk over some "beer mug" or "shandy-gaff," the last addition to our "bag," with the chances of the next "kill." The arsenical soap was mixed in the proportion of a handful to each quart of water, the whole stirred up into a good lather, and then well worked in with the paint brushes. This preparation effectually keeps skins from rotting or becoming tainted from the attacks of flies or other insects for any length of time, while the hair will remain on in perfect preservation; but it has the drawback of rendering the skins stiff and crackling, nor can they be easily afterwards made soft and pliable by any other curing process. A very weak solution of "carbolic acid," being one wine glassful to one hundred ditto of water was a common application, with very many other prescriptions and preparations.

The common native plan of merely rubbing in ashes from a wood fire, or "rak," as it is called, does well for a short time to keep the skin until it can be properly cured on return from the hunting expedition, and is certainly better than leaving it untouched, when the sun, or contact even with its own folds, or other loose skins, will surely spoil it, the hair coming off in flakes. For very small specimens, such as birds' skins, &c., a mixture of five grains of "corrosive sublimate" to one ounce of "spirits of wine" will keep off insects.

The ground where skins are about to be put down should be well smoothed at first, and it is best to select a spot clear of large trees, for the roots near the surface of the ground often prevent the pegs being all fastened down; this mistake is not always discovered until more than half the trouble is over. The skins of course are laid down with the hair next the ground, and should be in the sun, so as to dry sooner, one whole day then being sufficient. If placed in the shade they will take several days, which is often a bother, when a fresh move has to be made, for leaving them behind is not always safe. If taken up before being properly dry, they will surely become tainted, and lose all shape or symmetry. If rain falls while the skins are yet pegged down, they should be well covered over, or the wet will certainly spoil them, by washing off the preparation, and making them sodden. It is very vexing to lose fine specimen-skins—common ones can be replaced. Too many knives, and the means of sharpening them, such as files, small grindstone, &c., cannot well be taken out with any hunting expedition, for the thick skins of all large animals soon render the best knives terribly blunt. Old worn-out table knives, with the point broken off short, or rounded so as not to slip through the skin by mistake, or make long holes in skinning, will answer famously. On pulling out the pegs, the holes round the edges of the skin can be beaten flat with a mallet on the inside, when they will no longer be seen.

All this trouble is really necessary, or the handsome trophies will be spoilt, or lost altogether. The claws on the dried skins were very apt to vanish, of course nobody knew how, but these claws hung round children's necks are considered by the natives as charms against all sorts of evils. So the large dew claws and those of the fore paws had better be taken off before pegging down, if required to be kept. They make pretty ornaments when set in gold!

To preserve the skull of any monster tiger, it was cooked in an iron pot, and well washed white. After being thus boiled, the four large canine teeth will come out easily. These, without the skull, may be all that is required to keep. They, too, can be set as ornaments. Many of these teeth are perfectly hollow, while others are solid heavy ivory, irrespective, this matter seemed, of the tiger's age or size.

On skinning a tiger, the men seemed eager to secure, as charms against evil, the two clavicle bones. These are curiously bent, small bones, about four inches long, embedded in flesh and muscle, but disconnected with any other bone; where the fore arm is set on, they were called "gooj-bul," and were only to be seen in tigers, panthers, or lions. No doubt other smaller animals of the cat tribe may have something of the kind, but it seemed mere gristle.

Care had to be taken that no one burnt off the dead tiger's whiskers or bristles round the mouth, for this is done on the plea that otherwise these stout hairs might be used for poisoning some one, after being chopped up very fine, and so given in food. This superstition was a very general one.

The tiger's fat was collected and poked with sticks into bottles, and then melted in the sun; this was considered a most valuable cure for rheumatism by all classes! Some of the meat would be cooked, too, and eaten by the natives, as it was supposed to render them very valiant! Once a very petty chief, in a state of opium, wanted to hack a perfectly dead tiger with his sword for some purpose, but was stopped just in time spoiling a very fine skin.

It was difficult to tell any full-grown tiger's age, except by its enormous size, the faintness of the stripes—many of these being double ones, or opening in thin lines, on their flanks chiefly; also from the discoloured appearance of the teeth, like an old hound's fangs. The native idea about the number and size of the lobes in the liver, a fresh lobe being considered as added for each year's growth, was no criterion for judging of the beast's age, besides being very difficult to count, but about twenty years by common report seemed to be the full average age.

CHAPTER XII.

TIGER SHOOTING.

CAMP IN THE WOODS—FISH SHOOTING—BEES—CARRYING HOME GAME—FIRING THE JUNGLE—ANOTHER ACCIDENT—STUNNED TIGERS—A LUCKY ESCAPE—ODD ANIMALS OF DIFFERENT SORTS—PIGEON SHOOTING OR GUN PRACTICE—INDIAN TROUT.

OFTEN while encamped on the banks of a river in some jungly spot, herds of cheetal would come down to drink close to the tents of a morning and evening, but we seldom fired at these deer, for fear of disturbing the country yet to be hunted over, unless the men complained of being short of food. On arriving at any new ground, we made it a rule to abstain, as much as possible, from firing at any small game, unless something was absolutely required for the pot, when either a few green pigeons, flocks of which are be found in all large jungles, or a hare, which by turning out all hands to beat the bushes, could generally be got after going a few hundred yards only, or, perhaps, a big "murrel" fish was shot, for many a chance of finding large game has been lost by sportsmen attempting to combine a search for samber, cheetal, &c., in the cool of the morning, intending to hunt for nobler game in the heat of the day. However pleasant and tempting it may be, while merely strolling a short distance before breakfast to knock over a fine pair of horns, still the practice had best be avoided, for this is the very time at which bears and tigers, after prowling about all night long, are returning to their respective lairs to lie up for the rest of the day. On hearing shots in their neighbourhood, which has perhaps not been so disturbed during the rest of the year, they naturally betake themselves to other covers, a few miles off, well knowing that such an unusual noise betrays the presence of their great enemy the hunter, who, to his surprise, on visiting all the most likely places about, during the hottest time of the day, can find nothing but stale prints. He curses his bad luck, and wonders why the beast, of all the days in the year, and of whose whereabouts he has been assured, should have chosen that particular time to sleep elsewhere, and as he moves on hopelessly to hunt over fresh ground, the game thus passed over quietly returns to its accustomed haunts.

Talking of shooting fish sounds rather odd, but in India it is a very common practice, and is thus done. The native quietly secretes himself on some bank or tree overlooking any river or lake in which "murrel" fish are known to be plentiful, taking care to keep well out of sight, or the fish will not rise. Presently one of these big murrel, for they are often over two feet long, will slowly rise to the surface, and having emitted one bubble of air, will as slowly descend; this process is repeated every five minutes or so. Aim is taken at the fish's head, and no sooner has the matchlock ball struck the water, than, with a great splash of its tail, the fish disappears. The marksman instantly dives down after it, and begins groping about with his hands and legs in all directions, when the fish is mostly found, lying stunned and motionless among the tangled weeds at the bottom. Having grasped it well, he rises, and flings the slippery prize far on the shore, for it soon recovers, and if not found at once will swim away.

These fish are very common ; they look like mere logs of wood as they float on the top of the water, while often they are almost concealed under some large water-lily leaf, so a good look-out is required. The odd thing is, the bullet need not actually strike the fish to stun it if fired close to its mouth or head, for I have for fun, in about a quarter of an hour, shot at, dived for, and thrown ashore three monster fish of this kind, not one of which bore any marks of the bullet. These "murrel" are good eating, being firm, white fish, and nice change of food.

There is but little chance of starving in the woods, with the abundance of game of all sorts, including even peafowl; for far away from any villages there is not so much objection made to shooting them, if absolutely required for the pot. Honeycombs are often found, and will be presented to the hunter. There are two sorts; the smaller comb, often no larger than a small plate, is very frequently taken, and is by far the best honey. These are seen hanging among the leafy boughs of low trees, or in the middle of thick bushes, a long ball-like cluster of very minute bees, that can be easily driven away by blowing on them hard, and gently shaking the small branch while gathering it, when the whole harmless swarm having been dispersed, the twig with the comb can be broken off. These small grey bees seldom sting, but the other large wild bees had better not be interfered with, for they are most dangerous and vicious to a degree, so greatly dreaded by everyone. These bees turn out on the slightest provocation, such as smoke from wood fires, or the noise of people and animals passing near their nests. Several times I have known our small encampment in the woods completely routed by these pests, and have been nearly blind for a whole day on two occasions, yet the Bheels used to knock down, with long bamboo poles tied together, the immense combs of these bees, many of the nests being quite two feet long, and as many wide; often ten or twelve nests would be seen side by side hanging from under ledges of high, steep rocks, and other inaccessible places. These men of the woods, covered only with a black blanket, used to hold up on long poles burning sulphur to the combs in the heat of the day, and then knock them down (on the bees having dispersed), filling several large earthern vessels or "chattee" pots to the brim with the rather coarse, dark brown honey. Woe betide anyone accidentally passing near at the time, for on one nest being so touched, all the other swarms or hives would turn out in defence, filling the air for a long way around with the loud humming noise of their angry bees, ready to attack any moving thing.

In spite of the mischief tigers caused to the cattle of these villagers, the people at first were often very unwilling to admit that any such beast was known to be in the neighbourhood; and a good deal of questioning and pumping would be required on coming to a new place before it could be discovered that any bullock had been lately killed thereabouts. This feeling arises from an idea many natives entertain, that if a tiger is merely wounded, or even gets away unhurt, still he will be revenged on his informers or their cattle. Besides, among some, the tiger seemed to be considered rather a sacred animal than otherwise, until, perhaps, a man-eater appeared! A "faqueer," or holy beggar, once indignantly declared we had shot his horse on which he used to ride nightly, the same being a very old large tiger!

Again, I have heard one reason given for not disturbing tigers known to live in certain ravines near large towns, that they prevent thieves and highway robbers also lurking therein, but cannot credit this assertion, some religious nonsense being more likely the real cause.

Talking over strange ideas and customs, while driving a large ravine on one occasion, a tiger was heard to roar at something; on coming to the spot, we found a man, very emaciated, lying down under a shady, rocky ledge, close to some water. This poor fellow, being very weak and ill, had been carried there and left to die, far from any habitation. The tiger, on passing close by, had merely roared at him, but done no harm. We tried to persuade the men to carry him home, but to this proposal he strongly objected, so was left alone.

At another time, a tiger having been started on a rocky, steep hill-side, presently a terrific amount of roaring from several voices was heard; on going to the spot, it appeared that this tiger had attempted to enter a cave in which two large bears were already lodged. These bears positively refused to clear out of their hiding-place, so the tiger, after much prolonged growling from all concerned, had to pass farther onwards, when he was viewed and shot. Hearing the noise of the guns, the two bears turned out of the cave, when one was also killed dead, and the other got off badly wounded. A large, very quiet camel we possessed was sent for to the bottom of this hill, and after blinding its eyes with a thick cloth, we managed to load up both the tiger and bear, one on either side of the camel, when they were so carried to the tent, some distance off, to be skinned at leisure.

A precisely similar load was once more placed on this same camel's back, at a month's interval nearly, at another part of this grand hunting country. On the first occasion the camel decidedly objected to approach the dead game, but was persuaded to do so after some coaxing; on the second attempt it made no objection whatever.

Camels merely require to be carefully and kindly treated, when a good one can be persuaded to do almost anything, or go anywhere, kindness being the sole means with such a big, powerful, obstinate brute at times. One I possessed for years would allow firing off its back, and would wade through a wide, deep river even, when carrying three black buck besides the driver and self with gun and rifle; while, as an instance of endurance, I have travelled on the same camel, with a heavy driver, 244 miles in three days' time, being eighty-one miles per diem, resting it from 9 a.m. till 3 p.m. for food, and from 8 p.m. to 4 a.m. at night for sleep.

Sometimes, but not often, on account of the difficulty of extinguishing the flames, we set fire to any small isolated patch of grass jungle in which some tiger, wounded or otherwise, had taken refuge, and refused to turn out of, by any other means. This always had the desired effect at once, but the people were very averse to fire being employed, for it was so apt to spread in any high wind, and destroy for miles, perhaps, the immense crops of dry grass they so carefully preserved for feeding their numerous herds of cattle during the rest of the year, until a fresh crop of grass had sprung up.

A good opportunity of observing the terrible dread wild animals all have of fire was afforded me in the case of a monster tiger, whose back had been broken by a single rifle shot as it trotted past at no distance. This tiger on being hit instantly fell flat forward, while the rest of the hind part of its body and legs were dragged powerless behind. While watching it in this helpless state, suddenly a small column of smoke arose, the men in the cover behind having fired the jungle. No sooner did the tiger observe the smoke, than it began making frantic efforts to drag itself along the ground by its fore legs, constantly looking back, with raised ears and most anxious expression; so to put it out of pain I gave it another shot in the head.

The jungle on fire is a grand sight, and at night very pretty, as the long lines of fire are seen blazing over any distant hills, showing their outline to perfection, while the cracking of burnt timber, grass, &c., and the loud explosions of hollow bamboo clumps, make a noise enough to clear out every head of game over any extent of country for months to come, leaving the forest covered with black and grey ashes, about two inches deep, resembling so much snow to walk over. It is no joke sometimes to be caught in the woods on fire, if wishing to go in a contrary direction, for an opening is not always to be readily found in the wall of flame, while the smoke is stifling, and heat intense. Following close behind some grass set on fire we were once just too late to save a fine skin of a defunct tiger, that had gone away wounded; the flame had singed off completely one side of the tiger's skin, and so spoilt it.

Once as evening was fast coming on, and I could not get a wounded tiger to show himself, or move out of a dense patch of grass and bushes, the men set the place on fire. Thinking this tiger must certainly be dead, for it had been hit several times, I walked just behind the flames; suddenly, at my very feet, up sprang the tiger, from between two low rocks, where it had been hidden from the men on high trees around, and quite safe from the numerous bullets fired into all likely spots on speculation for an hour previous, as well as volleys of stones slung in by the men with their slings, in the hope of rousing the beast. The loud sudden roar of rage it gave on jumping up nearly knocked me off my feet, being so very close; it seemed to go in at the soles of my boots right through me, and out of the hunting-cap, like an electric shock, the effect being most staggering for the moment, and never to be forgotten; but I managed to fire one more shot through the smoke at the retreating tiger as it bounded off; and on looking round next morning we found it dead, not very far from the place. The two rocks between which it had been hiding were well scored with white bullet-marks, showing these animals know where to seek safe shelter on needing it.

On another occasion a tiger, with a broken fore arm, was known to be lying-up in a patch of willow bushes, not above four yards square, but nothing would induce him to show himself, though he roared constantly as shots were fired, and big stones flung at him from a high bank above, many of the stones being covered with thick bundles of dry grass set on fire before being hurled down, but the cover was too green to burn. At last, after I had cut down with bullets the green boughs all round this tiger, expending over thirty shots in so doing, all was quiet. On going up to look, he was found dead, killed by an accidental shot on the top of the head, for no part could be seen to fire at, his whole body being jammed between two high ledges of rock, that perfectly sheltered it from balls and stones. The place was scored all over with lead-marks, and I was on the point of leaving this tiger in despair, having no more ammunition at the time, and knowing from his loud roars up to the last that he was full of life. Only one long shot had been fired at him while sneaking off, but from the manner he held up his fore leg, I knew it was broken, but the whole cover was too thick to see more, when at length he was found to have taken up this position and refused to move on, when "band" beaters and self came up with him.

This is one of the cases where an elephant would have been invaluable, but none were to be had in that particular part of the country at the time. A few other tigers got clear off from time to time for want of an elephant, especially when they were found out in wide open plains covered with high grass, and only a few low bushes at intervals. Here the hunter on foot was helpless, for nothing could be seen, even two yards ahead, while of course one knew the crouching tiger could observe your every movement, and each advancing step, and so be able to choose his own time for attacking you unawares. Luckily, the country being chiefly hilly and rocky ground, enabled one to meet these animals with advantage on foot, and at a very trifling cost, which was a great point in those days.

With regard to hilly ground, it is very dangerous to attempt to follow a wounded tiger going up-hill, for there must clearly be a great deal of life left in the beast, or it would not face the extra fatigue of climbing, so the best plan is to make a wide circuit and trust to finding the prints or blood above, and then take them on, being in no hurry to follow too quickly. Better let him lie up somewhere and get stiff, or show by his course the point of refuge he is making for. Many accidents have happened from a charge down-hill, when weight alone tells, for no amount of good shooting can stop such a wonderfully heavy brute.

Once a very old tiger that we had wounded and lost was heard of about a week afterwards; he had gone to lie up in a large low cave or hollowed-out place under a big rock close to a piece of water, within one hundred yards of a village, where people at all hours of the day came down to fill their water-vessels. His foot-prints were seen on the edge of this water for some days, and caused much talk, but it was thought a tiger had merely come there to drink at night, and then gone elsewhere. Presently he was discovered by some one going to dig sand in the cave. Some natives then shot him, but not without his causing some mischief to the bystanders. This tiger had merely a broken arm, and two of our bullets were cut out and sent to us with the news of his death.

To show the unlikely sort of places tigers will occasionally lie up in during the heat of the day, I once, while travelling, traced the fresh prints of a large one (found crossing the high road), into a mere clump of shady trees close to a village in Southern India. In this small grove two men were busy cutting down a large tree, while women passed to and fro, filling water-pots from a well in this little thicket, of about fifty paces square only. These people were warned of their danger and sent away; but the woodcutters (perhaps disbelieving it) persisted in resuming their noisy work, whereupon a friend, who had meanwhile come up, again tried to make them leave the spot, until our men and spare guns could join us; for we had only a rifle apiece. During this last loud altercation, the tiger, with much rustling of the dry leaves, suddenly came trotting out on my side of the cover, and was shot forthwith; this being the sole occasion I ever knew of any sound being made by a tiger's footsteps.

Here is another extract from the book on "Tiger Shooting in India," written in 1857, with the object of bringing to notice a new description of repeating rifle, which was patented by the author, but could not then be brought to perfection, though in these days of hammerless guns and central fire brass cartridges, it would perhaps be more feasible than in the times when caps and nipples were needed, and when conical bullets, even, were doubted!

Cornet E., 1st Bombay Lancers, had ridden out from Camp Neemuch two days before to join me in a hunting expedition. While beating an open space of ground with only slight cover, E. and self both climbed a small thorn-tree, with our guns, to enable us to overlook the high grass around. Scarcely had the beaters commenced, when a fine tiger appeared, slowly walking straight towards us. We silently agreed to let it come on close to our post before firing, when a man who had climbed up a high tree beyond our position, called out most unnecessarily, thinking we had not observed the tiger's approach. This made the tiger stop and stare round for a moment, when it bounded off in an opposite direction. We instantly had to fire both our double rifles, and well knew our shots had told by the tiger's loud growls, but these long, hurried shots were all we could take before it disappeared in the high grass. The beaters now came up, driving before them a small tiger cub, which was rolled over with a single bullet, but managed to hide itself at the time in the thick grass, though it was found dead there two days afterwards.

As evening was coming on, we did not like to waste time looking for this cub, but at once began following up the blood of the big wounded tiger, which we took through thick bushes for about three hundred yards, keeping all the men well together, while we led the way. Presently we came upon an open space, but here all traces of the tiger suddenly ceased. Placing a man or two up trees to look out all round, E. and self advanced a few paces in front of the beaters to more minutely examine the ground for foot-prints before they should be obliterated by the feet of so many persons following us. While thus engaged we were startled by a loud roar from a small ditch a few paces on our right. At this time E. was stooping down about twenty yards on my left, busily employed in looking for the lost traces. The roar was instantly followed by the tiger, that came charging down at great speed, straight for me. I had barely time to fire both barrels of my rifle at only two or three paces at most, into her chest, when these shots, or the smoke, caused the beast to swerve past me and make straight for E., whom she at once sprang on, literally before he had time to get his rifle ready. The next moment I saw him falling backwards under the tigress, which was growling and roaring over him fearfully. My "shikarrees," with admirable coolness, now quickly handed me spare loaded guns; I instantly fired two more shots behind the beast's shoulder as she stood over poor E., but they had little effect, for she at once commenced dragging him backwards by the upper part of his left arm, which she had seized in her jaws, down a gentle slope towards the ditch in which she had been lying hid. The ground was very uneven, and covered with broken rocks, so I greatly feared to again fire, lest my friend should be hit instead of the tigress, for his face was touching her head, so no clear, steady shot could be taken at her brain, as she bumped him over these rough stones. E. had fainted while the tigress was thus carrying him off. She continued growling, and looked full at us all the time as the men and self followed at about eight paces distance. At last, after watching and aiming several times in vain to get a clear shot at her head (for it would have been useless to have fired at any other part), there was a chance, when my ball struck her on the top of the skull, whereupon she at once dropped E., and rolled over dead on the top of his body, bringing her open paw down on his chest. I quickly gave her the other barrel, and then ran in, with the rest of the Bheels, and pulled out E. by his legs from under the tigress.

While she was dragging him off the men were greatly excited. On the tigress first charging there was, as usual, a general move backwards for a step, whereby many were upset, but they immediately followed in a body, and much wished me to let them attack the tigress with what arms they had, such as swords, spears, iron-bound clubs, axes, &c.

On lifting him up, E. became sensible, and asked for water; he was quickly supplied with a long drink from the "chagul," or leathern water-bag. His arm, which was frightfully bitten, was at once bound up in a long turban, while the men busied themselves in cutting down small trees, from which, with a general contribution of turbans, waistcloths, and slight green boughs, a sort of litter was formed, and then we all set out for "Rajghur," about two and a half miles off, through the jungle, followed by the rest of the men, carrying the dead tigress, which was a very fine stout beast.

E., on being first seized, had a narrow escape from a blow aimed at him by the tiger's paw, which he fortunately guarded off with his raised rifle. The stock of the rifle was marked with her claws, while the guard and triggers were knocked completely flat on one side, so that the gun was useless until repaired. The tigress only dragged him about twenty-five or thirty yards, and the whole "scrimmage" was over in three minutes or so. From lying hid so close in the deep ditch, the men on the look-out up trees had failed to observe her. A "kole balloo," or old jackal, accompanied this tigress and trotted on before us while following up the wounded animal. A "doolee," or army litter, was quickly sent for from Camp Neemuch, and E. carried home therein, quite thirty miles. In course of time, he almost recovered from his wounds. This tiger was afterwards found to be singed with gunpowder all over the chest, so close did she come to my rifle barrels.

To show how uncertain a head shot may prove, unless fired so close as to be perfectly sure, on two occasions I have dropped tigers, seemingly quite dead, firing while they were standing quite still, and taking a long peering look at all they could see of me hidden behind bushes, as their custom is when trying to make out any doubtful object in their path. Both shots were about fifty paces off. I fired, fearing these tigers would wheel round and be off with a bound out of sight, as often happens. On walking up with the men to one of them, when within twenty paces, it got up and staggered on its legs, to our great surprise. Two more shots, given at once, killed it outright. The first shot was exactly between the eyes, so merely stunned this tiger for about a quarter of an hour. The other tiger, after lying flat on its side for some time in some low grass, got up with a roar, and raced off, and was not again seen, but on the spot, where there was much blood, we also picked up a broken tusk, so that brute also was merely stunned for a time.

Supposed dead tigers, and big game generally, should always be approached with rifles at the "ready," and spare guns close by, while some heavy stone or clod of earth is thrown and made to rebound from the carcase. More accidents occur from want of this simple precaution than almost any other cause.

Having beaten through the beautiful cover of "Bahara" (where so many animals had been found), on this day, to my surprise, it proved a "blank," for several cattle had been lately killed here. Wishing to explore all the caves of this ravine, so as to know how to act on any future occasion, with my men, I began looking into each cavern on passing. Presently, in the dark depth of a rather shallow cave, I saw something sparkling like a fire-fly at the far end. Silently pointing this out to my head "shikarree," he was some time before observing what it meant, for every now and then the dim greenish light would be somehow extinguished, when it would again shine forth clearly enough. We were whispering just in front of the cave, with the other men crowded behind, when my man gently pressed my arm, and muttered it was the tiger's eyes we were looking at! Rather a hasty retreat was made, for all saw by our manner that something unusual had been discovered. Quietly as possible we went round and climbed above the cave, when a sudden noise was made with stones thrown in the den, and pistol shots fired. A low growling just under our feet was heard in reply, when out rushed a big bear into the high grass and green reeds, which closed over him immediately in front of the cave entrance. I fired both barrels into his back, and on following up the blood he was soon found dead.

This bear was very old indeed, and very large; he had cunningly hoped to escape observation by remaining so quiet in the dark cave; had he rushed out at first, he might have upset the lot of us, no doubt mauling somebody, for there was neither time nor room to get ready and shoot him. Skinning him was a dreadfully tough job.

Next day we beat the long cover on the side of "Pawnghur" Hill Fort. I was posted on the edge of the steep rocky hill, lying down on bare open ground, so as to be just able to peep ever the rocky ledge. There was one doubtful

Maj. Gen. W. Rice, Delt. Shaw & Sons, Lith.

TIGER HUNTING.

open place between myself and the beginning of the long drive or beat, but a man was told to get up a tree overlooking this path, to turn back any animal attempting to leave the hill-side cover by it, though it was not likely that any would so try to break out above, the ground being so very bare, and rocks so hot. Directly the beat began I was delighted to hear the double blank pistol shots, that told of a tiger being on foot, but though the men had come close up to my post, nothing was to be seen moving in the cover below. The beaters, knowing I had not fired, very properly stopped advancing, but redoubled their noise, while keeping in a close body together.

All this time I was peering intently into the bushes just below the ledge on which I was lying down flat, in the hope of seeing some lurking tiger, when a slight noise, as if some loose flat stone had been trodden on and moved, was heard immediately behind me, whereupon quietly glancing over my shoulder I saw, to my horror, a very large tiger creeping most silently and cautiously past, within not more than four or five paces of my heels. The beast had evidently not observed me while thus lying down, though quite exposed, and so very close to him, for my reddish-brown clothes were, luckily, of much the same colour as the ground around. This tiger seemed only intent on moving off unobserved by the beaters, not far behind, and was slowly creeping past in the most stealthy manner possible, with his chin close to the ground and gaze straight ahead. (*See* Plate XI.)

For the moment I did not dare to even breathe, when to my intense joy, having passed on about ten yards, the tiger began to slowly descend a sloping path down the hill-side just beyond my post. The instant his head and shoulders were out of sight, with a feeling that it was impossible to remain still for another half-second, I sprang to my feet, and began firing the guns with the utmost rapidity into this tiger. On receiving my first two rapid shots, so intent was he on getting silently clear of the cover, that he turned sharp round, but merely uttered a long, suppressed, grating sort of gasp, instead of the usual loud, sharp grunt or "wough" tigers mostly acknowledge a hit with. My next bullet, about the shoulders, staggered him; in my haste and excitement the remaining shot missed, but the following one upset him, while the other guns prevented his again getting on his legs.

My men, hearing shots so close, all nimbly climbed up trees at hand, but on at length joining me, owned to being much puzzled at my letting the tiger go by, untouched as they imagined, for they well knew the very spot where I was lying down, and could not account for my not firing at it, little knowing that the beast had broken cover over the bare, open ground along the top of the rocky hill as described. These men all agreed that my escape had been a most wonderfully lucky one, and attributed it to my not having moved in the slightest degree, as well as to my whole dress being so much the same colour as the ground. My guns were all turned the wrong way, and placed under me as usual (to keep them cool), when the tiger passed in rear, so there would not have been time even to use them, considering how very close he passed me. His foot-prints clearly showed his course, yet, but for the accidental moving of the flat stone he had stepped over, this tiger would most likely have escaped altogether. He measured eleven feet ten inches, and was very stout and old. The man ordered to guard the pass or slight path over the hill had chosen to join the rest of the beaters, instead of climbing the tree indicated, and by this gross negligence had caused the mishap.

On another occasion, a tiger got past me alone, in much the same manner, but not nearly so close, and, being seen in time, the "battery" was quickly brought to bear on him, when he was killed. After being actually stuck up a certain tree, a man had failed to stop there, and so left a path unguarded, by which this last tiger very nearly escaped free—a great breach of duty, but these errors will occur. Extreme caution is the only safeguard after or close upon big game, together with the most perfect silence, with the acquired habit of moving about, when necessary, not in a jerky, sudden, quick manner, that is sure to attract attention, but very cautiously, and with a silent, cat-like tread, the brightest possible look-out being kept all the time, and the rifle never an instant out of hand; while no cover, however small or unlikely-looking, should be supposed impossible to hold a hunted tiger, for they will flatly crouch down in quite low grass even.

Some sportsmen allow their "shikarres," or gun-carriers, to also fire at big game on any supposed emergency, but this contingency I have luckily never witnessed, and have not the faintest trust in it, believing such a practice, at any time, greatly tends to increase whatever danger there might be, and is of mighty little effect as a rule. Of course the hunter must not expect to have it all his own way with big game. Several times I have had to make the very best use of my legs to escape a mauling, chiefly from bears; and this, no doubt, will be the case with others, in spite of the very superior weapons now used. Blank days, too, must be looked for (often in a long string or series), but they help to give a zest to the next "kill." Every one on first shooting in India is supposed to get "tiger fever," or an intense longing to be at "stripes'" death!

The above are some of the incidents to be met with while after large game; they do not comprise a tenth part of the various kills met with by the author, or recorded in the above-mentioned "Tiger Book," but will be quite enough to give any new hand an idea of how to go to work at first, when his own experience will help him on afterwards most successfully.

The largest "bag" made in one day was five large tigers killed, and a bear wounded. All these five wounded tigers had to be followed up at once by three friends and self, three being luckily soon found dead, and the other two discovered shortly afterwards, and duly accounted for, but not before our stock of ammunition had nearly run out, so a good supply in a spare case should be always taken to the field. Twenty-four rounds or cartridges could be carried in my own "shikar belt," which was cut out of soft, pliant samber skin leather in one piece, and somewhat resembled a waistcoat, being seven inches wide, with three girth-buckles in front, a broad back-piece, coming wide over the shoulders, affording great protection from the sun, and support to the waist (like the native "cummerbund)," most necessary for much camel-riding work. Everything requisite could be carried on this belt, without the chance of forgetting any essential in a hurry, while the weight, from being so well distributed, was not felt. A small telescope and hunting-knife were on either side, and there was room for a small metal grog flask (glass ones were constantly breaking). This belt could be worn without a coat, if needed, and there was no fear of articles dropping out during severe chases, tree-climbing, or other violent exertion.

The sportsman in his wanderings in the woods will meet with very many curious animals, but as this is not a Natural History Book, there is no need to describe them at length. The lynx is common in places, especially in Kattywar. I have seen them sometimes, in one long, tremendous bound, pounce upon a hare out feeding of an evening in an open space near the bushes in which the lynx had been hiding, and, after a little scuffling and dodging about, the hare was pretty sure to be caught. The hind legs of the lynx show tremendous power for springing. These animals used to frequent the patches of high grass where the florikin abounded, and many birds fell victims to them and the wild cats, as would be proved by the heaps of feathers found in places.

I have also seen hares that had been caught by large falcons; these birds used to take the hares up on to the top of big cactus bushes, and there feed upon them, having a clear view all round, or to be out of reach of jackals, perhaps.

The "Civet cat" will be met with but rarely; they go in parties of four or five, and used to be seen in the dried-up beds of what had been large rushy lakes during the rainy season; but in the hot weather, would be one tangled mass of dry broken reeds and flags, with wide cracked mud-clods to walk over. These spots hold grey quail in quantities. The "tree cat," "menuri," is very rarely seen, being nocturnal in its habits, living in the hollow trunks of trees. The Bheels sometimes brought them to be looked at as curiosities.

The "flying squirrel," common in Southern Indian forests. The "badger," or "beejoo," said by natives to dig out graves. Small "hedge hogs," very similar to English ones, only smaller. "Porcupines" are very common in places, but, being night wanderers, are not often seen; they also hide in burrows and caves.

The "mongoose," everywhere very common. I once saw a fight going on between a mongoose and big black cobra (in the open plain, as it occurs naturally), and have always regretted not having waited to see the end properly fought out. With all his bristles wide out, the mongoose ran backwards and forwards, without stopping for a moment, in a half-circle of about three yards length, while the cobra, tightly coiled up, excepting about eight inches only of its neck uncoiled, followed these movements regularly, with its head bent down and hood fully extended. With a beater, I sat down and watched this performance for more than a quarter of an hour, but as the mongoose had made no attempt on the snake all this time, I lost patience, and fired at the snake, the ball, missing its moving head, went through the hood, and we could plainly see the little hole of the bullet therein, but even then neither party discontinued their same monotonous movements. Presently, hearing the gun-shot, some one came up, thinking a deer had been killed, when the mongoose shut up his bristles and ran off into a bush, while the snake, uncoiling itself, began to crawl away also, but another bullet cut him nearly in two. No doubt this mongoose was trying to tire out the cobra, when so unluckily disturbed. I have seen a mongoose suddenly rush down a tree and catch a common grey squirrel feeding a little way off, much in the same manner as the lynx pounced on the hares.

The "Indian otter," also common, but rarely to be seen, from its habit of diving at the least sound. Once we saw a pack of quite eighty, big and little otters, altogether, leaping and running over the large dry stones forming the bed of a river, dried up in the hot season. They were evidently migrating to some other deep river close by. As they scrambled along, at a good pace, they uttered a shrill squeaking kind of noise. The "spotted wild cat," very common in Kattywar, as the ordinary wild cat is in other parts of India. The "desert fox," some few of which I saw while hunting for lions far beyond Deesa Camp, on the river "Loonee," towards "Balmeer" desert. This fox was of a reddish colour, like our English one, with a large white tag or tip to his brush. To make quite sure I rolled one over with a bullet, so as to be able to properly examine the specimen.

The "Indian scaly ant-eater." These curious alligator-looking animals are rarely met with, though in Kattywar they seemed not uncommon One coiled up asleep in a rocky sand hole, was pointed out to me as a monster snake! but a bullet in its course through the animal's head and body cut out the extremely long tongue at its base; on drawing out this tongue full length, I was gravely assured nothing could save my life after touching such a venomous matter! Another caused a watchman, or sentry, an illness from fright, feeling sure he had hacked a ghost with his sword! This animal, when dark, came out of some ruined stone well, and used to run down to a stream to drink water, and return at the quick shuffling pace they usually travel. These awful circumstances were duly reported to me, no one guessing what the apparition could be, but the foot-prints at once explained the matter, and next evening a charge of shot doubled up the ghost, when two rather deep sword-cuts were plainly visible across the wide scales on its back. These creatures are about four feet long usually; but I once saw at Camp Dharwar another sort, found in the jungles of Southern India, which was not quite two feet long, but seemed fully grown, with a very short, thick-set body, looking like a dwarf ant-eater. It was alive and newly caught. It does not appear in any books as an Indian animal that I have seen. The tail was very short.

The newly-arrived sportsman will hear, too, alligator stories. I have known a pet dog taken away while drinking water, within two yards of where his master and self were talking together on a low bank. The alligator covers himself in the mud, and so is invisible—goats, deer, and small animals suffer from them. Snake stories are frequent, but being painful subjects to dwell upon, shall be here omitted.

The gunner in India will find plenty of opportunities for keeping his hand in, for at all the stations and camps pigeon-shooting matches constantly take place, and some really good shooting will be met with. The pigeons used are invariably wild ones—"blue runt" looking birds, freshly-caught by nets at night down wells and other places, where they roost in numbers, and the birds are strong on the wing. In these days of "glass ball," &c., shooting, such small results are not worth mentioning; but the author may, perhaps, venture to state that he once won two cups in three days at two camps—travelling between each station, fifty miles on a mail cart, and the same distance back (equal in point of fatigue to more than twice as far on horseback)! At the first match, nineteen birds had to be killed without a "miss," and at the second, fifteen birds. Both matches were at thirty yards' rise. Six traps. Hurlingham rules; gun used—a pin fire, No. 12, double Westley Richards. There is a good deal of luck in pigeon shooting, for every one knows how birds will persist in dying just a few inches out of bounds. Still the above will show the average Indian shooting. These birds were the rather small dark blue "Indian stock-pigeon," caught the previous night by netting the front of large caves and rocks, to which these birds resort to roost, far out in the wildest part of the forest jungles, consequently wild, and strong enough on the wing.

The only people from whom the sportsman need expect to derive any assistance in looking for large game are the wild tribes, or those dwelling near large forest tracts. These men are invaluable, and truly brave, while their knowledge of all wild beasts is perfect. For small game shooting, every camp or village will supply men sufficient to act as beaters; but for sporting purposes the rest of the population, especially those dwelling in large towns, are worse than useless; moreover, nothing will persuade them to attempt anything of the kind. There are a race of wandering people called "Wagree," or "Pardee," the hunter will occasionally meet with; they are most expert at catching all kinds of small game, netting many deer out of herds of black buck at a time, and snaring pea-fowl, hares, bustards, florikin, and partridges, quail, &c., by scores. They can imitate the various calls of most animals or birds in the most marvellous manner, by voice alone. I have met these gangs of poachers with a live black buck or two, bound on the back of their bullocks, being carried for sale.

Apropos of these antelope, now and then a white "black buck!" is seen, also a doe, and these animals have not always red eyes. The news of a white buck having been seen anywhere travels fast, and there is much hunting for the prize, for they are very rare indeed. The so-called white is only a very faint light fawn colour after all.

The natives, in the woods, often manage to catch quantities of fish by damming up one end of a stream where it is shallow, and then throwing in a quantity of cut-down "milk bush," or "toor," at the same time beating the water as they wade in line down the stream, with boughs of the same poisonous bush. This causes the fish to turn up stupefied on their backs, when they are at once caught and placed in baskets, being none the worse for eating afterwards, as these folk declared. Women and children would all assist at these great catches.

A small trout was to be had in many of the streams in Rajpootana, rising well to the fly, and in every respect resembling the English trout, except that the spots were black instead of red. These fish were pink-fleshed, and from that cause called "goolab mutchee," or rose fish. I have heard of eighty such small trout being pulled out in a morning by a good rod, with the "black gnat" fly, not far from Camp Neemuch. The largest of these trout was about half-a-pound, but mostly smaller.

While snipe shooting on large lakes I have more than once seen the fallen birds taken down by big "murrel" fish a few yards from the shore, before they could be retrieved from the deep water. But here, in mercy to the reader, the drag must really be put on to these otherwise endless jungle incidents.

FINIS.

APPENDIX.

ANIMALS' NAMES REFERRED TO IN THIS WORK.

English Name.	Latin.	Native Names.	Page
Ant-eater, scaly.	Manis pentadactyla	Bajar-kit, Sillu. Kauli manjra.	218
Antelope, or Black buck	Antelope Besoartica	Hurun, Kalleea Kala hurun. Kalweet, Boorka.	82
Four-horned antelope	Tetraceros, Quadricornis.	Chouka, Jungleebukra, Chousingha.	103
Ass, wild	Eguns Onager	Ghor-khur, Ghour, Khur-Ghuddrey.	145
Badger, Indian	Mellivora Indica	Bijoo	217
Bear, black, Indian	Ursus labiatus	Bhaloo, Rinch, Reech, Aswail.	83
Bison	Gavæus Gaurus	Junglee Khulga Gaur, Ban-para, Maiss	108
Boar, wild Indian	Sus Indicus	Soor, Kala Janwur Dookar, Kok.	49
Buffalo, wild	Bubulus Arnee	Junglee bhyns, Arni. Ran-hela, Arna.	79
Cat, wild spotted	Felis torquata	. . . . .	218
Jungle cat	Felis chaus	Junglee Billee, Manjur	218
Civet cat (Lesser)	Veverra malaccensis	Mushak-billee Jowadi-manjur.	217
Cheeta, hunting	Felis Jubata	Cheeta	78
Deer, gazelle	Gazella Bennettii	Chinkara, Kalsipi Kalpunch.	41
Barking deer	Cervulus aureus	Kakur, Junglee Bukra, Bekur. Goontra, Beekree.	105
Hog deer	Axis porcinus	Para	102
Mouse deer	Memimna Indica	Pisai, Pisuree	106
Samber deer	Rusa Aristotelis	Samber, Meroo, Para	95
Spotted deer	Axis maculatus	Cheetal, Pussoo Chitra, Jhank, Kakra	65

ANIMALS' NAMES REFERRED TO IN THIS WORK—*contd.*

English Name.	Latin.	Native Names.	Page
Dog, wild . .	Cuon rutilans . .	Junglee Kuta, Bankuta, Kolsun.	79
Elephant . .	Elephas Indicus .	Hathee, Pheel . .	182
Fox, Indian . .	Vulpes Bengalensis .	Loomree, Kokree .	16
Fox, desert . .	Vulpes leucopas .	. . . . .	218
Hare, Indian . .	Lepus ruficaudatus .	Khurgosh, Sussa .	15
Hedgehog . .	Erinaceus micropus .	. . . . .	217
Hyæna . . .	Hyæna striata .	Jurruk, Turas, Nar Lakhar-baghar.	162
Ibex . . .	Ovis cycloceros .	Urial, Koch . .	103
Jackal . . .	Canis aureus . .	Ghidur, Shial, Kola .	190
Leopard . .	Felis pardus . .	Cheeta-bagh, Tendwah, Bimptee, Deep, Ara-wagh.	72
Lion . . .	Felis Leo . .	Sheer, Unteea bagh . Sawuj, Sooee.	136
Lynx . . .	Felis caracal . .	Siagosh . . .	216
Monkey . . .	Presbytis Entullus .	Lurgur, Hunaman . Bandur.	129
Monkey, Madras .	Macacus Radiatus .	Bandur . . .	129
Mungoos . . .	Herpestes griseus .	Newul, Newala, Mangus.	217
Nyl-Gai . . .	Portax pictus . .	Roz, Nylghaee, Rooee	48
Otter . . .	Lutra-nair . .	Panikuta, Jul manjer	218
Porcupine . .	Hystrix leucura .	Sayi, Sayal . .	217
Squirrel, Flying .	Pteromys petaurista .	Pakya . . .	217
Tiger . . .	Felis tigris . .	Sheer, Bagh, Nar Putait-bagh, Wagh	146
Wolf . . .	Canis pallipes . .	Langa, Bheeria .	78

APPENDIX.

BIRDS' NAMES REFERRED TO IN THIS WORK.

English.	Latin Names.	Native Names.	Page
Bustard, Ind. . .	Eupodotis Edwarsii .	Oom, Ghoran, Mhaldook, Khaldook.	12
Houbara, Bd. . .	Ortis houbara . . H. Macqueenii.	Oobarra. Tiloar .	12
Brahminy duck .	Casarca rulila . .	Chakwa. Surkhab .	22
Mallard . .	Anas boschas . .	Nil-sir, Buduk. .	25
Widgeon . . .	Mareca Penelope .	Charaz . . .	26
Florikin . .	Sypheotides Auritus .	Teluree. Khur-mor . Likh. Tunmor. Tekla	9
Geese . . .	Anser cinereus .	Hans. Haj . .	28
Jungle fowl . .	Gallus Ferrugineus .	Jungle-murg . . Ban-murg.	181
Kullum . . .	Grus cinerea . .	Koolung, Koonj .	40
Black partridge .	Francolinus vulgaris.	Kala teetur . .	7
Painted partridge .	Fr. pictus . .	. . . .	6
Grey partridge . .	Ortygonis Ponticeriana.	Teetur, Gorateetur .	7
Peacock . . .	Pavo Cristatus . .	Mor. Taus . .	8
Grey quail . .	Coturnix communis .	Butteer, Bahera, Lowa	4
Sand grouse . .	Pterocles exustus .	Butur-bur . . Puttooree.	8
Snipe . . .	Gallinago scolopacinus.	Chaha, Surkhab . Choonch walla.	17
Spur fowl . .	Gallopodix spadiceus	Chota-Junglee . . Murghee Kokatri.	182
Teal . . .	Querquedula crecca .	Chota Buduk . .	20
Cotton teal . .	Nettapus coromandelianus.	Girja Girri . .	21
Whistling teal . .	Dendrocygna ausaree	Silli . .	21

THE patent referred to at page 208 consisted of a gun or rifle, with two barrels placed over and under one another, soldered together and fastened at the breech ends into a socket A. Through this socket a large oval rather flat-shaped screw B, about three inches in diameter, traversed at right angles to the barrels. This flat-shaped screw B, being much pared above and below (parallel to its thread) to save weight, was bored completely through in three or five double sets of chambers, each set corresponding in bore and position with the two over and under gun barrels. This male screw B, fitted its female socket A most accurately, so perfectly that on the gun being fired there was no escape of gas or gun-powder smoke, even between the chambers and breech end of the barrels; this accuracy of fit being secured by the screw shape of the set of chambers B and its socket A, in which it traversed with a slight rotary movement, either to the right or left, being thus moved laterally by the action of a small half cog-wheel C, worked backwards or forwards in a half circle by means of a rack and pinion. Each of its four (or two only for a six chambered screw) cog-teeth fitting into a corresponding set of deep grooves, cut below each set of chambers in the screw B. This cog-wheel C was attached at its axis to a loop-shaped lever D, placed just in front of the trigger guard. Into this loop D the fingers of the right hand were thrust for the purpose of drawing it downwards, lever fashion, for about three inches, when on being released it at once flew back to its original position, being acted upon by a strong spring. The act of drawing down this lever had a threefold effect, for it raised and set on full cock both the "tumblers" or strikers of the two gun-locks (these being attached by long "swivels" to the mainsprings), at the same time causing by the teeth of the cog-wheel C, the now empty or fired set of chambers to traverse or pass on until the next pair of chambers were opposite the barrels, and on being released it securely bolted or held firm the whole screw B by flying up, as just described, into a bolt hole E, cut for the purpose through the socket A; one such bolting hole being below each set of chambers. The gun being at first cocked by hand (for the locks could be worked independently also, as in all guns), was held at the "present" precisely as any other fire-arm, there then being no need to take it from the shoulder until all the six or ten chambers were fired. Both triggers of the first two chambers being fired, the right hand left the bend or "hand" of the stock, and pulled down by an overhand pressure the lever D as far as it would go, instantly releasing it and re-grasping the bend or "hand" of the stock, ready to pull the triggers for the next set of chambers now brought opposite the barrels, and so on until all were in turn discharged. The sling rifle belt, with the double twist already described, supported the left arm, placed well forward while holding out and aiming the gun. All the chambers being fired (which could be done most rapidly in half second time for each shot), those empty sets protruding on the right side of the gun are refilled with central-fire brass cartridges, when the lever D is slightly depressed sufficient to set the screw B free from the bolt E, so that the whole set of chambers can be slided or twisted back to the extreme left. This exposes the last fired set of chambers ($\binom{9}{10}$ or $\binom{5}{6}$), and admits of their also being reloaded from the left side of the gun. To protect the protruding chambers from dust, rain, &c., and prevent the cartridges falling out, they are covered by a light thin moveable metal cap, that takes off and on, and is fastened by a spring catch to the gun. The extra weight of metal about the breech prevents any recoil from this gun or rifle. To save the left hand from the great heat of the barrels (after several rapid discharges) they are embedded in wood all over, except on the upper part whereon the "sights" are aligned. On the right or off side of the barrels, a light steel cleaning rod was fitted in between them and the wooden stock, the jag, worm, &c., being held in a trap in the butt of the stock. A very rough model of this invention (but with caps and nipples, central-fire cartridges not being then invented), was placed in the Museum at Camp Poona, Bombay Presidency, in 1859. The trouble of carrying and cleaning so many muzzle-loading guns formerly required for big game shooting, set me to work on this idea of a repeating fire-arm, as well as to save the time lost in exchanging an empty for a loaded gun. Guns on the ordinary revolving principle did not answer for large game shooting, for I tried them in vain. The escape of flame and smoke at the breech rendered it impossible to hold them out steady with the left arm, besides obscuring the "fore sight" and object aimed at as well, while such very small charges only of gunpowder could be used, on account of the recoil of the chambers, that no penetration was obtained at the closest quarters even. If only a round ball was used, the screw set of chambers need not be more than two inches or less in diameter. These chambers cannot recoil and can be easily lubricated outside.

N.B. Modern breech-loaders have rendered this crude idea of a repeating arm obsolete, even if it could be perfected.

W. R.